CARE AND VISITATION
MINISTRY
VOLUNTEER HANDBOOK

Care and Visitation Ministry Volunteer Handbook, Church Leaders Press

CARE AND VISITATION
MINISTRY

VOLUNTEER HANDBOOK

Equipping You to Serve

Scripture quotations are taken from the Holy Bible, New International Version. Copyright © 1973, 1978, 1984, 2011 by Biblica, Inc.® Used by permission. All rights reserved worldwide.

First Edition: Year 2020
Care and Visitation Ministry Volunteer Handbook / Outreach, Inc.
Paperback ISBN: 978-1-951304-32-4
eBook ISBN: 978-1-951304-33-1

CHURCHLEADERS
PRESS

Colorado Springs

CARE AND VISITATION
MINISTRY
VOLUNTEER HANDBOOK

Equipping You to Serve

Written by
Mikal Keefer

General Editor
Matt Lockhart

CHURCHLEADERS
PRESS

Colorado Springs

CONTENTS

INTRODUCTION

to the *Outreach Ministry Guides* Series

*Each of you should use whatever gift you have received to serve others, as
faithful stewards of God's grace in its various forms*
(1 Peter 4:10).

*T*his handbook is part of a series designed to equip and empower
church volunteers for effective ministry. If you're reading this,
chances are you're a church volunteer. Thanks for your willingness
to serve!

Several things make this handbook unique:

- The content is specific and practical for your given
  area of ministry.
- The information is compiled from experienced
  ministry practitioners—folks who've worked, served,
  and helped to train others in this particular area.
- It's written with you—a ministry volunteer—in
  mind.

Within these pages you'll find three sections. The first gives
a brief overview of fundamental principles to provide you with a
solid foundation for the ministry area in which you're serving.

Section 2 unpacks various skills related to the responsibilities
involved. Understanding what is required and assessing if it's a
good fit is helpful in creating a ministry team that is effective and
serves together well.

Finally, Section 3 provides a multitude of practical ministry tools. These ideas and tips will help you demonstrate Jesus' love to the people you serve.

Whether you're a first-time volunteer or a seasoned veteran, my prayer is that the information and practical tools in this handbook will encourage and assist you. May God bless and guide you in your ministry!

— **Matt Lockhart,** Project Manager

INTRODUCTION

to the *Care and Visitation Ministry Volunteer Handbook*

I'm not likely to forget Pastor Dale visiting me in the hospital, but not for the reasons you might think.

I'd been rushed to the emergency room by housemates who found me writhing in pain in my college apartment. The E.R. docs couldn't sort out what was wrong (it's still a mystery) but they weren't about to send me home in a VW van with a couple college sophomores who promised to nurse me back to health.

I was admitted and within a few hours Dale, a campus pastor, appeared.

Dale strode into the room like a spiritual field commander, quickly taking control of the situation. He led a flabbergasted young nurse by the elbow to the door, informed her he needed a few minutes with me alone, and closed the door in her face.

Dale then came and stood beside my bed, staring down from what felt like the ceiling. He'd come to pray for my healing, yes, but first a question: What sins did I need to confess?

In case, he suggested gravely, I didn't pull through. He was a former certified lifeguard who knew a thing or two about emergency medicine, and he had his doubts about my immediate future.

It all slid downhill from there. I was heavily medicated, but I don't think I'm imagining the nurse's return with a security guard. And I'm most certainly *not* imagining how dismayed the other patient (this was a two-bed hospital room) felt about being dragged into the encounter.

Oh, how Dale could have used this training manual.

From the moment Dale arrived, he did everything wrong. But as you take the advice you'll find here, advice from believers who've visited the sick in countless hospital rooms, nursing care facilities, rehab centers, and homes, you'll avoid each of Dale's missteps.

You'll discover how to embrace the *heart* of visitation, how to be spiritually prepared to usher peace and grace into every sick room you enter.

You'll learn how to connect with *everyone* in those rooms. Not just patients, but also the families and friends you'll find gathered at bedsides. Medical staff, too.

And you'll get practical tips that will save you years of learning by trial and error.

So, keep this little book handy—you'll refer to it often as you visit the sick *and* the healthy. Jot notes in the margins. Highlight what's most relevant to you today. See what questions arise and benefit from the answers it provides. As you share with other care and visitation team members, be open about what has gone well, and what could have gone better.

You're entering into lives at moments profoundly transformed by pain or fear, speaking with people who are spiritually open in ways they may seldom be open again. God will never be fully finished preparing you to be with his children when they're sick, suffering, or uncertain.

And make no mistake about it: God *will* be using you—even if, like Dale, you take a few wrong turns along the way.

It's an honor to visit God's children when they're sick or suffering; it's a joy to bring comfort to those so close to God's heart; and a blessing to knock on the door of a visitor who wasn't sure she was noticed, who was hoping she might make a friend.

While most of what's addressed here will refer to visitation of the sick, the skills are also applicable when visiting the lonely, the sad, or following up with those who have visited your church.

You'll gain the most from this book by marching through it as a care ministry team, pausing after each section to discuss the questions in Chapter 23. Your skills will deepen as a result, and you'll grow closer as a team.

Just remember: the ministry of care and visitation is a journey, one that will benefit others—and you.

God bless you as you serve.

— **Mikal Keefer,** Author

SECTION 1

CARE AND VISITATION
MINISTRY FOUNDATIONS

CHAPTER 1

WHAT THE BIBLE SAYS ABOUT CARE AND VISITATION

*W*hatever you do in ministry, it's wise to ask if there's a biblical foundation for it. With so much you *could* be doing, is this what you *should* be doing?

If you're about to call on, encourage, and pray for the sick and suffering, the answer to that question is clear and compelling: you're doing the work of God.

At least, according to Jesus.

When put on the spot and asked to rattle off the most important commandment, Jesus didn't skip a beat. He repeated a portion of the *Shema*, a prayer all observant Jews recited during morning and evening prayers.

> *"Jesus replied: 'Love the Lord your God with all your heart and with all your soul and with all your mind.' This is the first and greatest commandment." (Matthew 22:37-38)*

No surprise there.

What may have intrigued his audience was Jesus did not stop with the *Shema*. Instead, he added this:

> *"And the second is like it: 'Love your neighbor as yourself.'"*
> (Matthew 22:39)

In other words, loving God is critical, but so is your caring for people around you. You're not really doing the first without doing something about the second.

Love God, care for people. They're connected, two parts of a whole.

While visiting the sick isn't the only way to practically care for people, it's something Jesus talked about during his ministry. As he's describing the sort of actions that mark a faithful life, he says this:

> *"For I was hungry and you gave me something to eat, I was thirsty and you gave me something to drink, I was a stranger and you invited me in, I needed clothes and you clothed me, I was sick and you looked after me, I was in prison and **you came to visit me**."* (Matthew 25:35-36; emphasis added)

Of course, if we spotted Jesus suffering in any of those difficult situations, we'd rush to provide help. But Jesus isn't talking about caring for him personally; he's equating caring for other people with caring for him.

Love God, care for people—including sick and suffering people.

Jesus spent a significant portion of his ministry in the presence of people who were sick and suffering. He didn't shy away from helping those needing healing and comfort.

Were Jesus doing ministry on earth today, it's not a stretch to think he'd often be with those who suffer in a hospital bed, rehab facility, at home, or in an elderly care center.

Consider these encounters Jesus had with people who were sick...

> *Just then a woman who had been subject to bleeding for twelve years came up behind him and touched the edge of his cloak. She said to herself, "If I only touch his cloak, I will be healed."*

Jesus turned and saw her. "Take heart, daughter," he said, "your faith has healed you." And the woman was healed at that moment. (Matthew 9:20-22)

Which is easier: to say to this paralyzed man, "Your sins are forgiven," or to say, "Get up, take your mat and walk"? But I want you to know that the Son of Man has authority on earth to forgive sins. So he said to the man, "I tell you, get up, take your mat and go home." He got up, took his mat and walked out in full view of them all. This amazed everyone and they praised God, saying, "We have never seen anything like this!" (Mark 2:9-12)

A man with leprosy came to him and begged him on his knees, "If you are willing, you can make me clean."
Jesus was indignant. He reached out his hand and touched the man. "I am willing," he said. "Be clean!" (Mark 1:40-41)

Soon afterward, Jesus went to a town called Nain, and his disciples and a large crowd went along with him. As he approached the town gate, a dead person was being carried out—the only son of his mother, and she was a widow. And a large crowd from the town was with her. When the Lord saw her, his heart went out to her and he said, "Don't cry." Then he went up and touched the bier they were carrying him on, and the bearers stood still. He said, "Young man, I say to you, get up!" The dead man sat up and began to talk, and Jesus gave him back to his mother. (Luke 7:11-15)
Jesus went through all the towns and villages, teaching in their synagogues, proclaiming the good news of the kingdom and healing every disease and sickness. (Matthew 9:35)

A woman hemorrhaging blood. A man stricken with paralysis. A leper who falls to his knees as the crowd surrounding Jesus likely recoils in horror. Throngs of sick and injured pressing in on Jesus from every side.

And a dead guy.

A *dead guy*. That's taking "sick" to an entirely new level.

Jesus interacted with them all. He looked through their infirmities and focused on the people whose lives were held hostage by illness. He chose to care—and did so at a cost. In Jesus' day rabbis weren't supposed touch lepers. Getting in close proximity to a dead body meant being ritually unclean for a week. But Jesus still chose to show up and engage with those in need. He both reached out in concern and responded with compassion when he was needed by the sick.

So, yes: there's a Biblical foundation for serving in a care and visitation ministry. It's joining Jesus in service that was and is close to his heart. In fact, as he described the kinds of activities his faithful followers should do, he didn't indicate there was anything especially unusual about visiting the sick.

Of course, if you're his follower you'll be feeding the hungry, clothing those who need winter coats, and taking chicken soup to sick neighbors. That's what believers do as a matter of course. It's what love, kindness, and compassion look like when we see people in need and stop by hospital rooms.

The question isn't, "Is visitation the right thing to do?"

It is.

The question is, "How, then, should we go about it?" As you extend the love and comfort of Jesus to the sick, what's the best way to go about it? You're about to discover that the church hasn't always gone about it in precisely the best way.

CHAPTER 2

HOW THE EARLY CHURCH WENT ABOUT CARE AND VISITATION

The early church got a lot of things right.

There was life transforming, vibrant faith; a laser focus on mission; a heart for community that fueled widespread sharing and mutual support; and a love for God and for neighbors that shone brightly.

But when it came to practical nuts-and-bolts administration the early church discovered a few midcourse corrections were needed.

One of those appears in the Book of Acts, chapter 6.

The apostles got word Greek-speaking believers were grumbling about Hebrew-speaking believers, claiming Greek widows were being shorted during daily food distributions. Was the charge true? The Bible doesn't say, but the Apostles chose to not let the accusation fester. They called a meeting and informed the Jerusalem church that Apostles needed to spend their time preaching and teaching, not running a food program.

Seven trustworthy men were selected to administer the food distribution and life went on. The apostles preached, trustworthy men took care of logistics, and Greek widows got the food they needed.

No longer would the Apostles handle all the ministry done in and through the Jerusalem church. There was a world to reach and thousands of church members; it was impossible for a dozen men—apostles or not—to cover all the bases.

Later, the apostle Paul cemented the expectation that church members would embrace their individual ministries when he wrote this to the church in Ephesus:

> *"So Christ himself gave the apostles, the prophets, the evangelists, the pastors and teachers, **to equip his people for works of service**, so that the body of Christ may be built up..."* (Ephesians 4:11-12; emphasis added)

Paul wanted church members to actively serve and, as a member of your church care and visitation team, you're doing just that. Yes, your pastor may also visit the sick, but your service frees up your pastor to do those things that only pastors can do.

Your service puts you on the front lines of one of your church's most challenging ministries, one that will stretch you, keep you relying on God, and literally change lives.

In this guide you'll find tips, tools, and advice to make you effective and fulfilled in your service. And the first tip is one of the most important...

Connect with your care and visitation team

Sooner or later you'll find yourself sitting with someone who's dying, hugging someone whose heart is breaking, or speaking hope to people whose grief prompts him or her to lash out at you. Those are times you'll need to lean on others in your care and visitation ministry team, so get to know them. You're not just all doing a similar task; you share a mission, a ministry, and a need to support one another. And you'll not only need them—they'll need you, too.

Here's how Paul urged believers to relate as they served one another and the world:

> *"Be devoted to one another in love. Honor one another above yourselves."* (Romans 12:10)

When God calls you onto a service team—care and visitation, prayer, hospitality, or any other team—he's calling you to one another, too. Speak well of the other team members. Pray for them. Encourage them. Show up when they need you.

God has put you together for a reason.

"And let us consider how we may spur one another on toward love and good deeds…" (Hebrews 10:24)

Care and visitation is evolving constantly. What worked just a few years ago may not work today. What may be seen as a neighborly knock on the door in one community might feel intrusive in another.

Constantly ask how your team can be more aware of who would benefit from a visit. Explore fresh ways to get connected, including the use of technology. Follow up with people who received visits: what's their take on whether you were timely and helpful? What else could you have said or done? What shouldn't you have said or done?

"Therefore encourage one another and build each other up, just as in fact you are doing." (1 Thessalonians 5:11)

After a visit, connect with someone on your team to discuss how it went. What did you learn that might inform another visit? What did you discover that might help the rest of your team?

If you learn a hard lesson, let the rest of your team benefit from your discovery.

"…pray for each other so that you may be healed. The prayer of a righteous person is powerful and effective." (James 5:16)

As you engage in this ministry, cracks in your vessel begin to widen. Visits may drain you, giving you less emotional bandwidth to deal with challenges at home. You may find yourself struggling to sleep or focus. So pray for your team members. Ask God to heal what's hurting and bring into the light whatever needs to be forgiven and fixed. These are people who are on the front lines with you. They're in the battle, too, so come alongside them, starting with praying for them.

Does taking Paul's advice mean you and the rest of your visitation team will become best buddies? Probably not, but it does mean you won't function well if you remain strangers.

Get to know one another. If there's someone you think you can learn from, ask if you can buddy up on visits a time or two. If there's someone who's struggling, offer a listening ear and supportive shoulder.

As you go through this book, we recommend you do it *as a team*—taking advantage of the discussion questions in Chapter 23. They're not a quiz to make sure you've read the material; they're questions that will help you deepen your calling and coalesce as a team.

Bonding now means you're prepared when a tragedy strikes and you're tossed into the turbulent deep end of the pool. You'll know not just how to be with those who are hurting; you'll know how to support one another as you minister together.

CHAPTER 3

WHAT CARE AND VISITATION IS—AND ISN'T

*A*t first glance it seems that what you'll do in a care and visitation ministry is straightforward: you'll care, and you'll visit.

But let's say you get word that Terry, an elderly man in your congregation, has been admitted to the hospital. You slide behind the wheel of your car, drive to the facility and, after asking the volunteer manning the information desk for Terry's room number, you punch an elevator button and silently glide up a few floors.

Three minutes later you're standing outside what you trust is Terry's room. The door is partially open. Glancing in, you can see that someone—hopefully Terry—is in the bed.

You take a deep breath, whisper a quick prayer, and walk in.

But why?

To visit, yes, but why *exactly* are you there?

From the moment Terry was wheeled into this room, every other person coming through that door has had a clear reason for being there.

Nurses and aides appeared to administer meds, check vitals, and adjust equipment. A phlebotomist swooped in to draw blood. There was that lady with forms to sign. Doctors and medical students have poked and prodded, looking to fine-tune a diagnosis.

But you? What's *your* role in helping Terry find health?

Jeffrey Funk has walked through hundreds—thousands—of hospital room doors during his 30 years as a hospital and police chaplain. He's taught pastoral care and chaplaincy at Talbot School of Theology and trained pastors for visitation on multiple continents. Funk says you're there to come alongside Terry to give whatever he needs that's within your power to provide.

Which means you won't know exactly why you're there until you and Terry connect and he *tells* you why you're there.

"Visitation isn't coming in with a preplanned agenda or your assumptions about what patients need," says Funk. "It's not showing up to deliver what you already decided to say no matter what.

"You're there to be *with* patients. Everything that happens depends on what patients tell you they need. They may just need you to sit with them. They may need you to comfort them. They may need you pray with them and share scripture with them."

So whatever else you're doing in Terry's room, you're there to listen. Because you won't know what Terry needs until he lets you know.

In his excellent book, *Coming Alongside: Basic Pastoral Care at the Bedside,* Funk helps sharpen what roles you should—and shouldn't—fill as you make visits to the sick.

You're not a therapist—you're a listener

You'll connect with people on a remarkably tough day. They're sick or injured, likely experiencing pain and the harsh reality that the next few hours may change their lives forever.

Or even end their lives.

You may be tempted to help them process feelings they're not ready to face just yet—or aren't feeling at all. Funk recalls a visit he made that taught him a great deal about the value of pausing to listen and not playing therapist.

"Because I was a hospital chaplain, I had access to a list of patients and their admitting diagnoses. One particular woman had significant medical issues and I assumed she'd want to be comforted about those life-threatening challenges. So I went that direction and she went with me. We talked awhile and then I prayed with her.

"But when I finished praying and finally paused, she said, 'I need to share something else with you.' It was a serious family issue and I realized *that* was what was on her heart far more than her medical condition.

"She had a kid who was hurting and she was hurting for that child. That was her main issue.

"If I'd have rushed out of there, having done what I'd already decided to do, I'd have missed that. During our first 20 minutes together, I may have ministered to her.

"But it was the second 20 minutes that mattered."

Funk was fortunate—he had enough time to recover and zero in on what this patient really needed. Your visits are almost always going to be far briefer than 40 minutes.

And if you're with a patient for ten minutes, how thoroughly can you deal with a significant therapeutic issue anyway?

This isn't a call to avoid diving deep if that's where a patient wishes to go, but rather a caution: don't start what you can't finish or head into territory you're not qualified to explore.

You're not a medical expert—even if you are

One visitation volunteer serving in a Michigan church also happened to be a doctor working at a local hospital.

"Half the time I could do visits between seeing my patients," Tom says, recalling his years serving as a visitor. That was a plus of his taking on a volunteer role, as was his familiarity with medical jargon.

But there was also a huge negative.

"I quickly learned to never wear a lab coat or carry a clipboard when I was visiting," he says. "That just confused people. Was I there in my role as a health care worker or as Tom, their friend from church?"

And Tom's quick to point out a second downside to having his role misunderstood.

"Every patient had a team working to address their unique situation," he says. "That team knew far more than I did about the patient's condition, even though I was a physician. So when I was asked what I thought about a situation, I had to respectfully suggest that the questions be addressed to the patient's primary team."

Tom knew the medical team was covering their role and he needed to focus on his: providing comfort, a reminder of God's grace, and to respond to the spiritual and emotional needs shared by patients.

Even if you have extensive medical knowledge, it's unlikely you'll spot something the patient's medical team hasn't noted. But if you're confident you've observed something that might be of benefit and you feel compelled to share it, share it with the medical team—not the patient.

You're not there to lecture—you're there to connect

When Jeffrey Funk went to West Africa to help pastors deepen their visitation skills he discovered they had a lot of work to do.

"They didn't have a clue how to do ministry in a hospital setting," said Funk. "The local hospitals had big wards—ten beds to a room. The pastors' idea of hospital ministry was to stand at the end of the room and preach. And preach *loudly*. It was talking at patients rather than finding out what those patients' specific needs were or praying with them."

Patients you visit will seldom be hungry for a sermon. They're hungry for a listening ear and compassionate heart. You're there to connect—not lecture. Coming alongside a patient requires humility and awareness that God may have a different agenda for the visit than yours.

This training manual will equip you with a wide array of practical skills and tips from the visiting trenches. You'll be given a wealth of tools to take with you on your next visit.

But none of that matters much if you miss this: when you visit, *you're not visiting alone.* God is walking with you into those rooms and he's far more concerned with the hearts of those in the room than with your agenda.

So be open to connection. Connection with your own emotions, with the emotions of the people you visit, and with the Holy Spirit. It's the Spirit who'll quicken your intuition and help you make the most of your minutes with patients. It's the Spirit who'll steer you toward what's needed most, and who'll bring you joy in this ministry you've chosen to embrace.

SECTION 2

THE SKILLS OF CARE AND VISITATION

CHAPTER 4

THE ART OF LISTENING

*W*hile an undergraduate, David was both a starting guard on his college basketball team and a volunteer at a local crisis center.

"The center in East Lansing was a 24/7/365 operation," said David. "Volunteers worked three-hour shifts either talking with walk-ins or fielding phone calls. And when I think about which was harder—a day of running box-out drills, laps, and stairs, or actively listening for three hours—those shifts at the center were far, far harder. It wasn't even close."

If you've always thought of listening as just *not talking*, get ready to reconsider.

The sort of listening you'll do while making visits is the same sort that sent a collegiate athlete back to his dorm room to take a nap after three hours. But don't worry—we'll help you master the listening skills you'll find helpful as a visitor.

Dr. Phillip Hunsaker, a Management Professor at the University of San Diego, and Dr. Tony Alessandra, an author and speaker, suggest there are four general categories of listeners: non-listeners, marginal listeners, evaluative listeners, and active listeners. If you're to grow in this essential visiting skill, it's good to know where you're starting. Here's a quick description of each type of listener.

- **Non-Listeners don't put forth any real effort to hear what's being said.**

They pretend to listen and then quickly interrupt, preferring to steer the conversation and do most of the talking themselves. These people also tend to want the last word in any conversation about any topic.

It's unlikely anyone drawn to a visitation ministry would fall into this category, but it happens. Someone coming into a sick room with a prepared script to deliver—no matter what—would fit in this category. That person isn't there to listen, just speak.

- **Marginal Listeners listen—but only superficially.**

Mentally they ignore other speakers because they're leaping ahead, figuring out what their responses will be. They're also easily distracted by what's happening in the environment—background noise, what's playing on a television screen on the other side of the room, even their own thoughts.

This isn't someone who picks up on cues that a patient wants to talk about something specific, and these listeners often completely miss the point of what's said.

Something dangerous about these listeners: They often *appear* to be listening, but it's a mask they've pulled on.

Devon was having what he thought was a conversation with Aaron when Devon grew suspicious he was on the phone with a marginal listener. Aaron's responses—a sympathetic "I see"—came at regular intervals but never in synch with what Devon was sharing about his failing marriage.

"Every thirty seconds, like clockwork, I heard 'I see,'" remembers Devon. "So I tossed in, 'And that's when I stuck a banana in my ear and she…'

"Sure enough: right on schedule, an 'I see.' No mention of the banana. "Aaron was just waiting for me to finish so he could quote

Bible verses at me about divorce," Devon says. "We were never in a real conversation."

• Evaluative Listeners catch words, but not meaning.

These listeners try—they really do. But they evaluate what's being said strictly on the basis of words spoken, disregarding tone, body language, and facial expressions. By ignoring everything but the text, they often completely miss the intent of what they're told.

It's as if they're reading a court transcript, analyzing only words on a page. They've got facts, but not context, message but not meaning. The tragedy is that these listeners can often repeat nearly verbatim what was said so they're confident they've listened well. But people speaking to these listeners often walk away feeling misunderstood or even judged.

The truth is that in any conversation are multiple channels of information coming at you. One consists of the words used by the speaker. They're important: they carry that person's best efforts to describe a situation or feeling. The words chosen say a great deal about what that person wants you to know.

But that's just one channel a good listener tunes into during a conversation. There's also *how* those words are delivered: is it forcefully? Reluctantly? Without conviction? What emotion is communicated in the tone of the delivery?

The words, "I can do this," mean one thing when spoken on a high dive board by an Olympian competing for the gold and something else when stuttered by a knee-knocking novice standing there on a dare. Same words, completely different message.

Active listeners make sure they've captured the meaning of what's said by frequently paraphrasing what they've heard, checking to see if they've got the message right.

To the Olympic diver: "It sounds as if your experience gives you a great deal of confidence in your ability to make this dive." (Absolutely, I'm an expert.)

To the novice: "You seem afraid and like you regret taking that dare." (Yes, so please pull a fire alarm so, in the chaos, I can climb back down without jumping.)

Considering only the words someone says to you and ignoring the emotion means you'll miss most of the information available in a conversation. The approach is logical... but lacking. (And it explains why Star Trek's Doctor Spock was never invited to join a visitation team.)

• **Active listeners listen deeply, and focus on understanding the speaker's point of view.**

As our basketball player friend discovered, this sort of listening is hard work. It requires deep concentration and attention.

Active listeners don't judge the speaker's message but instead do their best to understand it. They pay attention to all the channels of information available: words, feelings, and thoughts. They set aside their own thoughts and feeling so they can give complete attention to the speaker. They also take note if the words said by a speaker don't seem to align with how the speaker appears to be feeling—those disconnects can spark conversation.

This sort of listener also is diligent to send verbal and nonverbal signals so speakers know they're being heard and understood. Not just well timed and in-synch nods and "I see" signals, but also summaries of what's been said so the speaker can either confirm or clarify.

The best-equipped visitation ministry volunteers are either active listeners or on their way to becoming active listeners.

So...where do you fit in that list?

Keep in mind most of us vastly overestimate how well we listen. If you truly want to know how well you listen, ask several people who know you well to rate you. But only ask if you're prepared to hear their answers. And if they think you've got room to grow as a listener, don't be discouraged—we *all* can improve.

The following are tips provided by active listeners. They'll help you listen more carefully, understand more fully, and connect more thoroughly.

Take time to practice

Listening is a skill, and one seldom taught in school. You can take classes that will prepare you to be an excellent speaker. In fact, many school curriculums require a speech class, but not listening. *That* you've got to pick up on your own.

Don't beat yourself up if you've discovered you've got some distance to cover. Instead, embrace the challenge and ask God to help you as you make strides.

Here are three ways to stretch your empathy and active listening muscles. Pick one and, along with another volunteer in your ministry, get in some practice time. You'll quickly become more adept at identifying what thoughts and emotions are being conveyed in conversations.

• Stream an emotional movie

You're looking for a film that's long on conversations and short on stuff blowing up. Pause the movie after scenes in which actors are in intense conversations and compare notes with another viewer: what were the actors feeling? How would you paraphrase what they were saying if you were checking with them for meaning?

• Watch a movie with the sound turned off

This helps you sharpen your ability to pick up on visual clues and to identify emotions. You should do the same drill with another volunteer: call out emotions as you see them play out on the faces of actors. Do you and your partner agree on what you're seeing?

• Talk with a partner about emotional topics

Do so knowing you'll be practicing techniques of active listening. The benefits: you'll find the phrases you use to check meaning ("I'm wondering if I have this straight..." or "So I hear you saying...") will grow less clunky the more you use them. You'll find your own ways of saying what needs to be said. Be sure to talk about emotional topics, not factual ones. Talk about the death of a childhood pet rather than your last vacation.

Relax

When people are sick or feeling overwhelmed by an issue in life, there's already enough intensity in their lives. Take a few deep breaths in the hall before going into a hospital room and let the tension drain from your body straight through the soles of your feet to the floor.

During your conversation feel free to glance away. Constant eye contact is, as we will discuss later, creepy. Don't let your presence add to the tension the patient is already feeling.

Don't listen alone

When you're making a visit, you're not doing it on your own. God is with you and the Holy Spirit will lead your conversation if you'll listen to him.

Skills are fine—and needed. But they're not everything. There's also being tuned into the nudge of the Spirit as a nuance in what's said (or left unsaid) catches your attention and you circle back to ask about it.

When you paused to relax outside the room you whispered a prayer asking God to walk with you, right?

Leave your agenda in the parking lot

"That's something I literally do at times," says Susan, a pastor who often visits cancer patients. "I jot on a pad of paper what concerns in my life are getting in the way of my being present for a patient. And I leave that list on the car seat. Those worries will be right there when I come back—I won't forget them."

She knows she can't actively listen if her mind drifts back to her own stuff while she's listening to others. Take a cue from Susan and keep a pad of paper and pen in your car.

Then use it.

Minimize distractions

Active listeners pull a chair up close to the person they're listening to, for several reasons.

First, it's just easier to talk when you're not shouting across a room, but another reason is that narrowing your focus to just the patient helps you listen better. You're not distracted by readouts on the medical equipment, a conversation in the hall, or that sparrow sitting on the window ledge.

You can't control everything, but if you've got a weakness for watching sports and a television is showing highlights of the playoffs, sit where you won't be tempted to sneak peeks. Better yet, ask if for the duration of your visit you can switch off the television.

But if the patient suggests you join him watching the program, then by all means do so!

Listen with your body, too

One important way to communicate you're listening is to *look* like you're listening. Lean toward the person you're visiting. Maintain frequent eye contact but not to the point you look like a hawk swooping in for the kill.

Kelly was practicing making eye contact while taking an active listening class through her church. She knew she was taking it a bit too far, she remembers, when a colleague at work who was sharing a story finally paused and asked, "Do I have something in my teeth? You keep staring."

You know you're pulling a Kelly when the people with whom you're speaking keeps breaking eye contact—or starts believing you intend to kill them.

Also, avoid checking your watch or a clock on the wall. Silence your phone and tuck it away.

How you sit matters, too: keep an open, inviting posture. No crossed arms or legs. Do your best to not fidget as you listen.

Be mindful of your facial expressions

A yawn will signal you're bored or too tired to pay attention. A frown sends the message you disapprove of what you're hearing. An eye roll in almost any conversation is deadly.

Do this: Wear a pleasant smile as you enter the room. Then, as you discern how the patient is feeling, mirror that emotion in your countenance.

Some visitors feel they're there to "cheer up" a patient, so they arrive with an arsenal of jokes and anecdotes about funny things that happen in hospitals. Almost always, it's a bad idea to attempt to entertain. Far better to initially take the emotional temperature of the room and reflect it back.

Engage mentally

Pretending to listen is a key skill for anyone who spends much time in school. Students master this skill because teachers can get upset if they catch students mentally napping or gazing out the window.

One way to not shift into Marginal Listener Mode is to picture what the patient is describing. Whether it's a literal story ("When I saw the pickup shift lanes I remember noticing the driver was looking down, maybe to dial a cell phone.") or a concept ("I just can't respect a God who'd let my mother suffer like this.") mentally create a visual of the event or word. It keeps you firmly in the moment and helps when it's time for you to make a comment.

Keep some phrases handy

It feels awkward using them at first, but this handful of phrases help you reflect back what you're heard:

"I'm wondering if I have this straight. Are you saying...?"

"So I hear you saying..."

"When you talk about how you've been treated you seem... [angry]."

"It sounds like..."

"It seems as if..."

"So you feel..."

"I'm curious..."

Any phrase that tentatively mirrors what you think you're hearing gives the patient an opportunity to confirm or clarify, and either response moves the conversation ahead. That mirror may come in the form of a question or with your simply repeating a statement made by the person speaking.

Ask follow-up questions

Follow-up questions build on something the other person has already said. For instance, "You mentioned this illness rocked your faith in God and I'm wondering if you'd talk more about that. What's that looked like?" Asking questions based on what the patient has said practically shouts that you're listening—and invites ever-greater depths of sharing.

Be okay with silence

It's exhausting being ill and even more exhausting preparing to die.

When Betheen was in her final hours, several visitors sat by her bedside. Since Betheen wasn't responding to their questions or comments, they assumed she was no long able to hear them.

They began chatting quietly, speaking across Betheen's prone body. Several minutes later, without opening her eyes, Betheen shushed them. "I need quiet," she said. "It takes a lot of concentration to die."

Sometimes your words—no matter how well intentioned—are just unwelcome noise. Be okay if that patient you're visiting prefers that you sit quietly with her, or even watch a movie together. Let the patient lead.

If your emotions get in the way, say so—then move on

When Doctor Tom was visiting a church member who said the only thing hospitals care about is money, Tom found his defensiveness and emotions blocked his ability to listen any further. Were some hospital employees motivated solely by their paychecks? Probably—but Tom knew many more who weren't.

So Tom cleared the air by reminding the patient that he, too, was a physician. And he added, "In every profession there are greedy people and I'm sorry you've run into some here. As a doctor I do my best to never be like that—but thanks for the reminder to be careful."

The key is to not to let hurt or defensiveness derail you—and to as quickly as possible return the conversation to the patient.

It's worth keeping a mental list of topics that are likely to snare you, too. What shuts down your ability to listen?

Explore feelings—carefully

If you pick up on an emotion, it's okay name it and see if it's something the patient is comfortable owning. You'll likely be corrected, but that's fine—you're getting greater clarity about what's happening in heart and mind of the patient.

You might say, "When you said this heart attack was unfair, given all the working out you do, you sounded angry. Did I hear that right?" only to be told that, no, anger isn't the right word. It's more "disappointed."

Whether the emotion is anger or disappointment you're still connecting when you rightly identify the emotion. It may be an invitation to explore that emotion more deeply. Again, you're not a therapist. But if you sense a patient wants to dig deeper, you might follow up with, "I'm curious: who are you angry with/disappointed in?" Now you're talking about God not meeting a patient's expectations, and you can speak about God's love for the patient no matter what the circumstances might be.

Don't interrupt—even to be of help

If you're listening well and the patient is exploring thoughts and feelings, you may hit spots in the conversation where the patient sounds confused, where sentences tail off unfinished. The patient seems to be struggling to find the right word.

Just wait patiently—don't interrupt.

What you're usually seeing is someone sorting out thoughts or feelings in real time—and that *takes* time. Rushing in to finish the patient's sentence may feel helpful, but you may be leading the conversation away from where it needed to go.

If you do feel compelled to interrupt, do so tentatively: "I think I hear you saying you're scared of this surgery—do I have that right?"

Wait for a natural pause in the flow of a conversation to ask clarifying questions. If there's something that was said earlier that you want to circle back to, just say something like, "You said something earlier that's stuck with me and I'd like to know more about that. You said…"

Remember that acceptance isn't endorsement

People believe all sorts of odd things about the Bible and God.

As a visitor you may hear beliefs expressed you know are flat out wrong, but unless those beliefs interfere with being able to connect with God's comfort and grace, this isn't the time to shift to a Bible study aimed at correcting biblical errors.

You're not in the room to judge anyone's biblical literacy. Stay on mission.

Save your solutions

When people share their challenges, you might want to jump in to save the day with a quick solution. Resist the temptation. You're helping someone discover his or her own solution, one far likelier to be implemented than anything you recommend. Plus, most of the challenges that might prompt your visit don't have any simple, clear solutions—at least none that are apparent after a few minutes of conversation. You'll be most helpful if you stay true to your calling as someone who's come to bring God's love and hope into the room.

Buy some peppermint oil

Here's one last practical tip from a visitation volunteer whose ministry was saved by a simple health food store purchase:

Mike always carries a small vial of peppermint essential oil in his car's glove compartment. "Some hospitals have an odor I find hard to be around," Mike admits. "I roll a bit of peppermint oil on my upper lip so I don't smell the background scents. It helps me concentrate."

Ken is in a similar situation. He describes himself as a "sympathetic gagger." If someone nearby vomits, he's guaranteed to join them. If he catches a whiff of a strong scent his stomach does a back flip. "I'm not the guy you want visiting you in a hospital," he says—so he stays far away.

But Ken employs his considerable listening skills in many other situations. He simply avoids places his gag-reflex will be triggered because he's aware he won't be an effective listener there.

Pause here and consider: are there situations in which you can't be effective? Are there triggers that bring past trauma or emotional images flooding forward in such a way that they shut down your ability to focus beyond yourself? If so, let the coordinator of your visitation team know so you're not sent somewhere you can't serve well.

And take note of the issues that came to mind. They're places in your life you may choose to explore further.

Learning about active listening is great—but the way to grow in this skill is to actually *practice it with intentionality*. No special equipment is needed. You've got what you need to become the best listener you know. Truly. What you may lack is motivation, so here are three reasons to grow as a listener:

• You'll become a better friend

Not just to those you visit, but to those whose lives you're already in. Everyone appreciates being valued and heard, and active listening helps that happen. As friends discover you're tracking with what they think and feel, they'll open up more. Mutual trust will grow. You'll have deeper, more meaningful relationships.

• You'll be more successful at work—and life

Why? Because giving feedback to be sure you understand others cuts down on misunderstandings and demonstrates a higher emotional intelligence—which is directly correlated with success in any situation requiring teamwork. You'll be more productive because you'll be paying attention and more attune to the emotions of colleagues, better able to read what's happening around you.

• You'll be happier

Active listening skills can be deployed to resolve conflicts, to grow closer to a spouse, to engage strangers, to observe a world you may have previously ignored.

So practice this skill. It will open doors and let you see through walls. In a world where confrontation is common and understanding increasingly rare, it's a superpower (though you have to provide your own cape).

CHAPTER 5

THE ART OF COMFORTING

*H*aving spent multiple pages emphasizing the need to listen well and speak carefully, it's now time to reveal a secret about visiting: Words are overrated.

Yes, they matter, but they often matter less than the simple fact of your presence. It's huge that you show up during a difficult time; it's even bigger that you do so demonstrating respect and compassion.

When Dale was a teenager he'd been part of a church youth group that was especially close. Dale had long ago moved away but, when he returned for his father's funeral forty years later, he found many of his youth group friends had come to stand with him at the funeral.

"I'm sure most of them said something comforting," Dale says, "But I can only clearly remember what one person said."

Following the funeral, a woman (let's call her Danni) kept effusing what a joy it was to have the gang back together again. "She was in full-blown reunion mode," says Dale. "But me—not so much."

At one point Danni literally pulled Dale away from a conversation with friends of his father to get him to pose with the rest of the now-grown youth group. "They were shuffling around nervously," Dale says, "But they knew better than to tell Danni to back off. She's a force of nature." All Danni wanted, she said, was to take one group picture, so Dale dutifully stood in the row while Danni positioned her phone. "Now everyone smile," she bubbled, "Especially you, Dale. Don't be a party pooper."

"My thought was that if ever there was a party that needed pooping, this was it. My *dead father* was literally at the front of the room," says Dale, shaking his head. "This was his *funeral.*"

Danni's presence—and how she misused it—was vastly more impactful to Dale than anything she may have said when she greeted him with sympathetic words. Physical presence is like that. It can amplify or erase anything you say. Besides, since you're visiting primarily to listen, you won't be saying all that much anyway.

As you become a more skilled active listener, your body language will also reflect the attention you're giving to the emotions of the people you're with. You'll gain the ability to read a room, to take the emotional temperature, and adjust accordingly.

But comfort isn't only about physical presence. It's also expressed in words you might say—and words you should *never* say. Let's consider a few candidates for the "Never Say This" list. Just like some words open the door for coming alongside a person in pain, other words can just as quickly slam shut that door shut. Here are a few phrases that all but guarantee a door closing in your face:

Comforting things to never say…never!

"I know how you feel"

No, you don't. Even if you've also lost a child, had cancer, or endured a financial disaster, your experience isn't the same as what the person you're with is experiencing.

If your intent is to build a bridge with the patient do this: Listen and empathize. Help the patient articulate how she's feeling and why. Stay focused on her, not your own stories.

"It's going to be fine"

Do you really know that? Your empty promise of a positive outcome dishonors any anxiety or uncertainty a patient feels. With five simple words you've made it unsafe to admit to anything but hope and confidence.

Even if you happen to be the world expert on whatever's wrong with the person you're visiting, you can't guarantee that everything will be fine. So don't do it.

"If you need anything, call me"

That *sounds* helpful, but it's actually handing a person who's hurting a difficult homework assignment.

First, that person may not yet know what he needs. He's caught up in the crisis of the moment, not thinking about what he'll need tomorrow, next week, or next month. Plus, when it does dawn on him that while he's in the hospital the milk in his refrigerator is slowly spoiling and his lawn is turning into jungle, he doesn't know if addressing those issues is what you meant when you offered help.

If the scope of your visitation ministry also includes providing ongoing support, be specific about what help you—or the ministry—can offer. If it's shuttling someone to doctor appointments, say so. If it's delivering groceries weekly, or showing up for visits twice a week, or making phone calls, say so. Be specific.

When her husband was hospitalized with a brain tumor, Jenn found herself buried under an avalanche of tasks. She still recalls with affection answering a knock at the door and finding her next-door neighbor standing there, his lawn mower sitting in her driveway.

"He told me that until Gerard came home, he'd mow our yard every week," Jenn said. "That was one thing I didn't have to worry about. He had it covered." Lawn maintenance hadn't even made it onto Jenn's list—there was so much else to worry about, so many other plates to keep spinning.

"He continued mowing for nearly a year," Jenn said. "It was a practical offer that he faithfully fulfilled, and he took the burden off me of thinking of things he could do for us."

"Give it time—you'll feel better soon"

Unfortunately, time doesn't heal all wounds. Not on its own, anyway.

Some wounds (a lost child, a ruined relationship, a marital betrayal) stay raw until healing comes, and that healing isn't on a schedule.

You'll be visiting people who may be coming to grips with a future that's now empty of what once gave their tomorrows purpose. Their future feels bleak; you're promising that more future will inevitably fix what's broken—and it's just not true.

" The Bible says God will never give you more than you can handle"

Actually, that's not what Paul writes in 1 Corinthians 10:13. He's addressing temptation, not illness, and the clear implication is that with God it is possible to resist temptations. Paul's message is true, but this verse may not be the most relevant one to share with someone dealing with illness or loss. In other words, beware of the temptation to apply Scripture out of context.

And that's another filter to keep in mind when you're choosing what to say or not say: Be sure it's true *and* helpful.

The fact that something you say is true is wonderful, but if the other person isn't willing or able to hear it, why share it? You're talking to yourself. Worse, you're preaching to a congregation of one person, someone who is hungry for help, not platitudes.

True and helpful: That's the gold standard.

Comforting things to say…so say them often

Even if your opportunity to offer comfort is measured in seconds rather than minutes, these are words that soothe and bring hope.

"I've been thinking about you and praying for you"

This is a declaration of support and comes with an unspoken subtext: "I see you. I honor your pain. You are not forgotten and you're not alone." These are helpful, hopeful assurances indeed.

"I'm sorry you're sick"

There's no demand for more information tucked into this simple comment. It's a quick nod of support that leaves the door open if someone wishes to talk about what's happening.

"How are you feeling?"

This is an invitation to talk about whatever elephant is in the room. It invites but doesn't demand. If this question is met with a polite but vague response, it's likely an indication the patient isn't up for giving you details. Respect that.

"Is there anything you'd like to talk about?"

This open-ended question gives patients permission to talk about anything and everything, including, if they wish, anything *but* their current difficulties.

Matt was in the midst of a messy divorce when his old friend, Andy, gave him a call. Andy was coming through town on business and wondered if Matt had a night free for dinner. Matt couldn't wait. For months he'd been neck-deep in the emotional muck of discovering his wife's infidelity, coping with lawyers, and watching his life unravel. An evening of respite shared with someone he'd traveled with, played pranks with, and laughed with since middle school sounded perfect.

Except before they were seated at the restaurant, Andy was asking about the marriage, suggesting Matt and his wife try counseling. Giving advice Matt neither wanted nor needed.

"I told Andy that we'd tried everything," Matt says. "I told him what I really needed was a night away from all the crap. I needed a night off.

"Andy stopped, took a deep breath, and said, 'Remember that time we handcuffed Ross to a refrigerator?'

"I laughed so hard that night I cried. I hadn't laughed in weeks. It was heaven."

Andy let Matt set the agenda—and the agenda was anything *but* Matt's complicated problem. Andy let go of his own agenda and listened well.

A word about comfort and touch…

A brief, reassuring touch on someone's arm or hand can bring immediate comfort to a patient. It signals that the patient isn't alone and that, in spite of unwashed hair or a lack of makeup, the patient is still approachable and acceptable. But touch is dangerous, too. It can send unintended messages. It can also be physically dangerous for a patient.

Make it a habit to always use a hand sanitizing station before entering a hospital room. In most facilities they're everywhere—and no one will resent your using hospital sanitizer to assure patient safety. It's routine practice for staff to clean their hands between patients. If you're unsure you'll find a station where you're visiting, carry a small container of hand sanitizer with you.

Because you'll often be visiting people you don't know well, treat them with the same regard you'd show them if they weren't in a hospital bed. That means a reassuring touch on the arm or a gentle handshake may be acceptable—or not.

If a patient offers a hand to shake, shake it. If you'll be praying with a patient it's okay to ask if the patient would like to take hold of your hand while you pray.

As for giving every one you visit a warm hug, don't do it even if you think of yourself as a "hugger."

What it takes to comfort someone depends on the person being comforted. Some people you visit will want physical contact and some won't. Some will look forward to hearing a cheerful story and some won't. Some will want to hear scripture read and some won't.

Take your cues from the person you've come to serve.

CHAPTER 6

CONFIRMING YOUR FIT

*W*hether you've already started making visits or you're preparing for your first, let's make sure this ministry is a good fit for you. Why? Because if you're wired for visitation you'll grow ever more comfortable sitting with people who are hurting, angry, or struggling to find hope. But if this ministry isn't a fit, you're headed for burnout. Maybe not immediately, but eventually.

So, what does it take to be a good fit for visitation?

Have the right heart

"There are plenty of individuals doing pastoral care work like visitation who are great teachers," says retired Colorado pastor and veteran visitor Rob Strouse. "They know all the right things to say to someone who's suffering, but that's not who'll be successful in a visitation setting. You're looking for people who have a shepherd's heart—who are sincerely moved by the pain others feel. They sense a responsibility and calling to visit with the sick, elderly, and hurting. They live lives marked by mercy and compassion. That's who will have the most impact while visiting." Does that mean someone who makes a visit out of duty rather than a deeply felt desire to do ministry is wasting her time? No, because God can use any visit to minister to those in pain.

But if people who know you well would say you're able to empathize with others, and you've earned a reputation for being compassionate and kind, then you're probably perfectly suited for this role.

Maura Barrett serves as the Pastoral Care Associate at St. Thomas Church in Delmar, New York. It's a role perfectly suited for someone with nearly 30 years of social work in her background.

Asked who's likely to thrive in her visitation ministry, Maura says, "I look for people who are positive, kind, and confident. Nobody's perfect in this ministry. We all say and do things that could be said or done better. We all get nervous. But if your care shines through, you'll be forgiven for just about anything."

Maura also looks for people who are comfortable talking—and listening. She seeks out people she says are naturally communicative and comfortable in their own skin.

And then she lets them take the ministry out for a test drive.

"Visitation isn't for everyone," said Maura. "I let people try it by shadowing several experienced visitors before they commit. That way, potential volunteers see there's more than one right way to make a visit, and they can decide if this is a good fit for them."

Have the right stomach

There are people who can't tolerate the sights and smells they'll inevitably encounter in health care facilities and sick rooms. Try as they might, they'll never be particularly useful making visits. For them, the heart is willing, but the flesh is…well, flip-floppy.

Tricia was diagnosed with Guillain-Barre Syndrome. During her several month hospital stay a parade of friends, family, and colleagues stopped by to see her. Including, now and then, people serving on her church's visitation team. One such visitor arrived when a friend of Tricia's was already in the room. The care and visitation ministry volunteer had brought her husband along; a man Tricia could tell wasn't all that excited about being there.

"He kept glancing around the room and never once made eye contact," says Tricia. "He was fidgeting, and paid far more attention to the tubes running into me than to me."

Tricia's friend took his cue when the couple arrived and asked if he could offer a brief prayer before departing. It was a prayer made even briefer when a "thud" sounded about two sentences in.

"The husband passed out cold," Tricia remembered. "Fortunately, he fell backwards against the wall and sort of slid down to the floor. If he'd gone face-first he'd have become a patient himself."

It was the last time that husband/wife team made a hospital call together.

If you're acutely squeamish about the sight of blood or the scent of a leaking catheter, consider serving in another ministry area, one where you'll feel more at home.

To be clear, you *will* be stretched during visits. There will be moments you're uncomfortable or unsure what to do next; that comes with the territory. And those are moments that can be transformative for you and the person you're visiting because they're the very moments you'll rely on God to guide you to the next word, the next touch.

But if you're likely to face-plant during a prayer, consider limiting your visits to non-medical situations.

Have the right spirit

When Rob Strouse is asked to describe the spirit of an effective visitation ministry volunteer, he pauses before finally answering.

"It's humility," he says, "That's the key.

"You go into the visit humbly, asking God to show up. Then you stay in the moment, listening not just to what the person you're visiting is saying, but also what God's telling you."

Because there will be times, Rob notes, where the person you're visiting can't tell you anything. He's too sick to speak, or she's in the final hours of her life and anything other than your prayer and gentle touch is simply a distraction.

That sort of spiritual sensitivity isn't a matter of training. It's a consequence of a volunteer's vibrant faith life, and willingness to follow the Holy Spirit's guidance.

So enter into the visitation ministry heeding the advice given before every airplane flight lifts off: In the unlikely event of a loss in cabin pressure, oxygen masks will appear, dropping from the ceiling. Before assisting others, first pull on your *own* mask. In other words, make sure you're spiritually well before attempting to assist others who are hurting. Minister out of your abundance, not your weakness.

If that's you, if you're wired to be present for others and to let God work through you to comfort his children, then welcome to a ministry that will deeply touch lives, including your own.

How your visits look and sound may shift from visit to visit. While the vast majority of tips and training in this book relate to visits made to the sick, but you may also visit the elderly, the widowed, those whose infirmities have left them isolated, or people struggling with finances, people who have mental health diagnoses, and the dying. One small book can't possibly dive deep into all those specific arenas, though you'll find some useful tools relating to each of those groups.

Rest assured that if you master the skills that make for effective hospital visits, they're completely transferable to when you visit struggling people who have no health concerns but face other issues.

Listening is listening. Respect is respect. Caring is caring.

Connecting with a patient who's exhausted while recovering from a significant surgery isn't all that different than visiting with a new mother whose baby hasn't let her sleep for several days. Both need encouragement, prayer, and hope that a better future is waiting.

You can be present for both the sick congregant and the new mother, and your humble spirit of service will bless them both.

SECTION 3

CARE AND VISITATION TIPS AND TOOLS

CHAPTER 7

HOSPITAL VISITS

*A*t the outset you need to know this: Hospitals *want* you to visit patients—for several reasons.

The first is therapeutic

A Journal of Health Affairs survey of 800 recently hospitalized patients and 510 physicians found that both groups agreed that compassionate care is "very important" to successful medical treatment. Yet the survey also revealed only 53 percent of patients and 58 percent of physicians think the current health care system generally provides compassionate care.[1]

That gap is significant in part because there's strong evidence that compassionate care improves health outcomes. Encountering compassion is so important that some health care leaders suggest doctors and nurses should be trained to provide compassion as well as being trained to set bones and take temperatures. Others recommend building more time into health care providers' schedules so there's a better opportunity to listen, give hope, and gain trust.

But making space for compassion is tough in a world where heath care professionals are constantly pushed to do more in less time. There's no margin for lengthy conversations when three more patients are waiting just down the hall.

---

1   https://www.healthaffairs.org/doi/full/10.1377/hlthaff.2011.0539

But *you* can deliver compassion. You're not a health care provider but you are someone who listens, and those hungry for a listening ear will take whatever ear is offered.

And then there's this: being in the hospital is boring

And bored people quickly become cranky people. Your visit provides a spirit-lifting boost, a bright spot in a day otherwise filled with tests, therapies, blood draws, and bed rest. You may be the only person in a patient's day that won't be poking, prodding, or pulling out a needle.

So you're wanted. You're invited in. Just remember that when you visit a patient in a hospital room you're a guest of not only the patient, but also the hospital. And a good guest follows the rules.

What rules? Each hospital has its own, but here are some general guidelines that will help you be a guest who's not only welcome, but also welcome back:

•Be sure a patient wants to see you

Many hospitals ask about visitors as part of the intake process. A quick call to the hospital information desk will let you know if your presence might be a problem. (The fact that you're a fellow church member doesn't mean you'll be viewed as "family" by hospital staff.)

• Park where you're instructed to park

Hospitals normally have parking facilities divided into spots reserved for staff, patients, and visitors, with the visitors having the furthest to walk.

That's not because medical staff think they're more important than you. It's to get medical personnel at their posts as quickly as possible, and to accommodate their 24/7 schedules.

Honor the parking signs and you'll not only have a little longer to pray as you hike to the front door, but you'll also find your car hasn't been towed while you were inside.

• Announce yourself

Check in at the front desk and then, when you reach the patient's ward, at the nursing station. You're sliding into the rhythm of the hospital providing care for the patient; be sure you're doing so at the right time.

• Respect visiting hours

They can vary from ward to ward, so call ahead and ask specifically when your presence is allowed. A hospital's website is also a great source of this information. Even hospitals that have open visiting hours are likely to have suggested visiting hours.

• Be flexible

Some hospitals restrict the number of visitors a patient can have at one time, so be aware that staff may ask you to wait until someone else leaves, or request that you come back at another time.

That's also one reason you'll want to carry with you a notepad or get-well card, so you can leave something for a patient who is unable to see you.

•Be healthy

To you it's a slight sniffle; to a patient with a compromised immune system it's a problem. Don't carry any germs into a hospital that can hurt the patient you're visiting (or anyone else with whom you come in contact).

Symptoms that are signs you should *not* visit include coughing, infections, fever, diarrhea, a rash, or vomiting.

• Wash your hands

Some hospitals insist all visitors clean their hands when they first arrive and provide waterless hand-wash pumps for that purpose. Even if no such rule exists, it's still a good idea. And it's just as good an idea to wash your hands when you're leaving so you don't carry any germs out of the hospital with you.

• If you bring gifts, bring the right ones

Most visitation ministries don't suggest taking gifts to patients, but if that's something you want to do be sure you've chosen wisely.

At many hospitals potted plants aren't allowed in surgical or high-dependency wards. Flowers may not be welcome in the intensive care unit. Food may be restricted, too. And if you do bring flowers, also bring a vase.

Instead of a gift that will require care, how about bringing something to read at 3:00 a.m. such as a positive, faith-based paperback? Just be sure the book is new, and not used, so you're confident nobody else was reading it while sick.

• Respect roommates

In a shared room all that separates you from another patient may be a thin sheet serving as a room divider. Everything you say will be overheard, so speak softly and be aware you have an audience who may be trying to sleep or rest.

• Take your cues from hospital staff

If someone in a lab coat or uniform swoops into the room to interact with a patient you're visiting, excuse yourself and head into the hall. Don't be offended at the interruption; be grateful the patient you're visiting is getting attentive care.

•Never touch medical equipment—as in *never*

It's sitting where it's sitting for a reason, and it's sensitive. One visitor discovered that scooting over a monitor to allow a chair to be pulled up next to the bed signaled the nursing station that the patient was going into cardiac arrest. When they burst into the room with a crash cart it was the visitor who nearly had a heart attack. And don't even *think* about adjusting the patient's hospital bed. They're more complicated than the space shuttle: things won't end well.

So you're in compliance with all the hospital rules, regulations, processes, and procedures. Now what? Here's a list of additional tips culled from the experience of seasoned visitors. Most of it was learned the hard way, so soak in the wisdom.

Before you make a visit...

• Double-check your data

Be sure you have the patient's full name and it's spelled correctly. Also have as much relevant medical information as possible. If your spelling is off you may be told Tom Smith isn't in the hospital, but had you asked about Tom *Smythe* you'd have gotten a different answer.

And speaking of checking your information...

• Call the hospital to confirm the patient hasn't been discharged

It's amazing how quickly patients are sent home following surgery, and how fast patients can be treated in an emergency room. Make it a habit to phone the hospital just prior to leaving for a visit to determine if you'll be making a hospital or home visit.

Some hospitals won't tell you if a specific person is a patient in the hospital. If you ask, "Is Jackie Johnson a patient?" you'll be told that information can't be released. Which makes sense: you might be the person who put her in the hospital in the first place. The hospital is simply protecting Jackie. But if you ask what room Jackie Johnson is in, you're likely to get the room number because you already know she's a patient. So ask the second question—it'll tell you everything you need to know.

- **If a surgery is scheduled, visit the patient the day before the procedure**

If you attempt to meet with the patient upon his or her arrival at the hospital, you'll just be in the way. Patients are often scheduled to arrive just in time for pre-op preparations, and their mind is on the upcoming surgery, not you. But the night *before* that surgery can be long and hard. That's when comforting words are most needed. That's where a reassurance of God's love can have a great impact.

That means you'll likely meet with the patient at home, not the hospital. See Chapter 9 (In-Home Visits) for some helpful tips.

- **Pray—several times**

Pray for the patient and your visit before you enter the hospital and again as you pause outside the room. Center your thoughts on God and commit yourself to being a vessel through which God can bring comfort.

- **Try to coordinate your visit with a patient's treatment schedule**

Many therapy treatments and tests tend to happen in the morning hours so you'd be wise to avoid showing up for a visit then. When contacting the hospital for information, ask if you can speak to the ward where the patient is being treated. The nursing staff may be able to recommend a time you should visit.

• If you're dealing with personal concerns, set them aside

Some visitors jot them on a pad of paper that's left in the car. Others mentally leave concerns in the hallway before they go into a room. You won't be an effective listener if your own issues distract you.

• Dress appropriately

This isn't a formal occasion, but neither is it a "come as you are" moment. Business casual usually sends the message you're taking this meeting seriously.

• Forgo wearing anything scented

This isn't the time for perfume or cologne that may aggravate allergies or cause distress for someone with a respiratory condition.

During your visit...

• Be brief

It's been said before but bears repeating: brevity is good. Patients are almost always short on energy; don't let your visit drain them. Also, some patients feel a need to rally and provide entertaining, interesting conversation. That's exhausting; let them off the hook by not extending your visit. The only exception is when a patient asks you to stay longer because there's something that patient wants to discuss.

• Consider making visits with another visitor

Some ministries make this mandatory, along with only visiting patients of the same gender. Other ministries don't have enough volunteers to double-team a patient or to take gender into consideration.

If you're visiting a patient of the opposite gender, consider asking a nurse to enter the room first to make sure the patient is appropriately attired to receive a visitor.

Whatever the policy of your ministry, follow it. If there isn't a policy, talk about it.

• Read and respect all signs

Before entering a hospital room read any posted signs. Is there a "no visitors" sign displayed? Oxygen in use? An isolation protocol in place? Anything involving radiation? Most signs involve medical treatment and won't impact how you go about making a visit. But some might so be sure you understand what they mean and why they're there.

Take signs seriously. They apply to you.

• Turn off your phone

You're thinking the "vibrate" setting will make your phone less intrusive, but it's far better to simply switch off the power before you walk into the room. That way, you're not tempted to check it.

If there's something going on in your life that makes it impossible to turn off your phone for ten or fifteen minutes, make your visit at another time. It will probably be impossible for you to focus on the patient until that issue is resolved.

• Knock before entering a room—even if the door is open

You're entering someone's bedroom so knock, announce who you are and why you're there, and wait for a verbal confirmation before entering the room. It's common courtesy and what you'd want to happen, right?

If a curtain is drawn, let it stay that way until the patient gives you the okay to pull it open or come to the other side. A bath or bedpan procedure may be underway.

• Don't wake sleeping patients

Some visitation ministries suggest checking with a nurse to see if awakening a patient is okay, but at least one hospital nurse recommends avoiding that conversation.

"A sleeping patient is usually a recuperating patient," says Dana, a nurse who's served most of her career on surgical floors. "I'd never recommend a visitor wake up a patient."

Dana points out the patient may have had a pain-filled night and desperately needs the rest, may have been awakened a half-dozen times because of critically-timed tests, or had a sleep cycle disturbed for another reason.

"Let sleeping patients sleep," says Dana. "And unless you have a medical reason or you're someone they've told us they want to see, don't let me catch you waking them up, either."

• Carry cards and a roll of cellophane tape

Someone's sleeping? Let the patient know you were there by leaving a note or card either just inside the room or lightly taped to the door.

• Read the room

When you enter, take note of what's been added by friends and family. If there's a carnival of balloons and banners, or a jungle of plants and flowers, it's likely the patient has a robust support group of friends and family.

But if there's no evidence of other visitors, the patient may be in this alone—and feeling it. A sterile environment is a hint that you might explore whether the patient is feeling lonely.

• Read the patient

As noted, you'll connect best if you're pleasant when entering and then quickly begin reflecting the emotional tenor of the room.

Knowing the patient's diagnosis won't necessarily tell you how someone's feeling, nor will his or her prognosis. But if the patient is staring pensively out a window, or laughing while watching a comedy on television, or there's an uneaten meal shoved to the side of a tray table—those are clues. They're also starting spots for making an observation.

"I noticed you seemed to be thinking as you looked out the window. I'm wondering what you're thinking about these days."

"You seem happy. Do I have that right?"

"It appears you don't have much appetite. Is there something that's bothering you that you'd like to talk about?"

Clues can lead to conversations.

Watch for signs of fatigue, too: yawning, eyelids drifting closed, a lengthy break in eye contact. If any of those are in evidence, wrap up your visit.

• Remember the other people in the room

You're there to bring hope and encouragement to everyone, not just the patient. Stay mindful that your visit begins the moment you walk into the hospital and isn't over until you're back in your car. Treat everyone you encounter with respect, empathy, and warmth—they're all carrying burdens you can't see.

If family or friends are in the room, introduce yourself and pause to sense if you've interrupted a moment of reconciliation or another emotionally charged exchange. If so, suggest you come back in ten minutes and go grab a cup of coffee as you silently pray for whatever is happening at the bedside.

If family is present and clearly fatigued, offer to sit with the patient while they visit the cafeteria and get a snack. Agree on a time they'll be back and settle in. If you and the patient talk for ten minutes and then the patient falls asleep, that's fine. You can pray for the patient until the family returns.

• Maintain a steady demeanor

The patient may look gaunt, have experienced significant weight loss, or have multiple tubes snaking in or out from under the covers. Do *not* react with horror or shock at what you see or smell when you enter the room; your response will almost certainly register with the patient.

• No hearty handshakes

You may be known for your sincere, knuckle-crushing grip while shaking hands, but trade that in for a gentle handshake in the hospital. A vigorous shake can disrupt IV lines—not something you want to do. Mirror the pressure the patient uses when shaking hands, and only shake hands if the patient offers a hand to you.

• Don't sit on the bed

Doing so both invades the patient's personal space and can also make the patient physically uncomfortable as the blankets tighten.

• *Do* sit where the patient can comfortably see you

Hospital beds aren't built for facilitating conversation so make sure you're positioned so the patient doesn't need to crane a neck skyward or to the side. Be mindful of being backlit by a wall of bright windows, too. The glare will be uncomfortable for the patient who's trying to make eye contact with you.

• Find out what's top of mind for the patient

It may not be his or her medical condition. When Dan got a text from his buddy, Craig, all Craig said was that his wife, Lynne, had been in a serious car accident. Dan hurried to the hospital and made his way to Lynne's room where he found Craig being wheeled out by an attendant.

What Craig *didn't* mention was that he'd been in the same accident and broken multiple bones, suffered serious lacerations, and had a laundry list of injuries. Craig didn't care about any of that. His greatest felt need was comforting his wife who'd not only been hurt but also lost her mother in the wreck. Visiting Lynne was what gave Craig comfort, so that's what Dan did. Checking in on Craig could wait.

• If you carry a Bible, make it a small one

Arriving with a brick of a Bible can be intimidating. It may signal that a full-blown Bible study is about to begin. But a pocket-sized Bible is far less frightening to anyone who's been pinned in a corner by a well-intentioned Bible student who felt the need to preach. If possible, bring a new Bible that you can leave, too, if the patient wants it.

• Look to share Scripture

You'll find some suggested passages in Chapter 20, but don't think you need to rattle off all of them. A few relevant passages that are soothing to a patient are far better than a barrage that don't quite fit the patient's situation. And don't feel you need to explain what you read. Let the Word of God do what it does best: find a pathway into the heart and mind of the hearer.

• Look to share the Gospel

Especially if a patient isn't a believer, this is a moment when a brief sharing of the hope that's in Jesus may be welcome. And if someone does believe, this is a time to remind him or her they're not alone and that God loves them.

But do be brief—if patients want more details, they'll ask.

• **Take this saying to heart: "If a doctor shows, out you goes"**

During your visit a nurse, doctor, or another medical staff may come into the room. That's your cue to promptly, graciously excuse yourself and leave. If either the staff member or the patient doesn't feel you need to go, they'll let you know.

• **When meals arrive, offer to leave**

It's awkward to eat in front of another person who doesn't have food. Don't put the patient in that position; excuse yourself so the patient can eat while the meal is hot. It won't taste any better if the patient lets it sit while you continue your visit.

• **Always assume a patient can hear you**

Even if the patient appears to be sleeping or you've been told the patient is in a coma, the patient may be able to hear you. Never say something while a patient is unresponsive you wouldn't say if the patient were alert and listening to you.

• **Don't assume patients are aware of their situations**

A patient may not be fully aware of his diagnosis and prognosis or may be in denial. Confronting him about his serious situation isn't helpful…unless it is.

"Chester was my father-in-law," says DeAnne. "He was hospitalized with stage 4 cancer and my husband and the rest of the family refused to accept he was dying. Whenever we visited, the talk was all about all the fishing trips he'd take once he got home and the cruise he'd book with my mother-in-law. Chester looked miserable through all those conversations.

"I went by myself once and I said, 'Chester, I think you're dying.'

"He said, 'I know, but nobody will let me talk about it.'"

Telling patients they're dying is *not* recommended—or seldom appropriate—but in this situation it was exactly the right thing to do. DeAnne had listened well and realized that Chester wanted to have a conversation but was unwilling to upset his family. She had the conversation privately and it brought great comfort to Chester and the chance to discuss spiritual matters.

"He died two weeks later," said DeAnne.

• Refrain from moving patients

Sooner or later a patient will ask for your help getting to the bathroom, or shifting from the bed to a chair. Don't do it.

There's an art to moving a person from one spot to another, and you haven't mastered it. It's very possible you'll do damage in your attempt to be helpful. Rather than agree, quickly offer to let a staff member know of the request and go get someone who's qualified to provide the help needed.

• Never force a conversation—or get offended

Yes, you made the effort to come visit. Yes, you've gone out of your way to come at once. You even paid for parking. None of that matters when you're visiting a patient. You're there for that person, not yourself. If the patient doesn't want to talk, don't talk. If the patient would rather you leave, graciously go. If the patient doesn't want to pray with you, don't pray with the patient.

You can only give what the patient is willing to receive, so don't push it.

Don't become offended by what a patient does or says. Medication changes people, as do fear and concern. You're with people on what may be one of the worst days of their lives; cut them some slack. Proceed with grace.

• During surgeries, offer to sit awhile with the family

There's often a family member or two counting down the hours in a surgical waiting room. Your being there with them can provide significant support. Be sure to identify yourself, greet each family member, and say something like, "This must be a difficult time for you right now. How are you feeling?" to see if the family wants to talk. That won't always be the case, but just your presence may still be appreciated.

If it's clear there's a family huddle underway, offer to share a quick prayer and be on your way.

• Know—and respect—your limits

Your role has already been discussed in detail. In the heat of the moment, when a patient asks you to cross one of those lines, don't waver.

Memorize this line: "I'm not someone who's equipped to do that, but I can do this: I can listen, learn, and share a hope that's meant a great deal to me."

• Be ready to make a referral

Talk with the coordinator of your visitation ministry to find out who you can suggest be contacted should a person you visit need support after being discharged. Is there a meal ministry? Is there a pastor or counselor available?

Do your homework *before* you walk into a hospital room.

More information about making referrals is in Chapter 19.

• Don't make promises you can't or won't keep

If you're not absolutely certain you'll be back, don't say you'll return. If your church's ministries don't provide support services such as meals, help with doctor appointments and the like, then don't imply those will be forthcoming.

Share that you're there now and that's what you can do.

After your visit...

• Keep confidences

There's a more detailed look at HIPAA (Health Insurance Portability and Accountability Act) issues related to visiting patients in Chapter 18, but here's a rule of thumb: what's shared during your visit is private. Medical information certainly, but also anything the patient shares about what she's thinking and how she's feeling.

An exception: if the patient talks about harming herself or others, that's something you'll need to disclose because the cost of not disclosing it may be too high. Speak with a medical staff member about what you've heard.

Check with your visitation ministry leader about existing policies related to your church but please: no posting updates online or sent through a prayer chain. No leaving notes about your visit sitting around the church office.

• Ask: Do you need to connect with a Pastor?

Sometimes theological issues arise during a visit that are beyond the scope of your visit, or that you simply can't answer. Rather than bog down during your visit, ask the patient if a visit from a pastor would be helpful. If that's true, pass the request along.

• Consider your condition, too

Serving in any ministry that enters into lives at hard times can take a toll. If you find yourself experiencing difficulty sleeping, or having a hard time navigating your feelings about visiting others, you may need a break.

Stay attentive to how helping others impacts you. After a call can you let go of the emotion after a reasonable time, or does it haunt you for days? Does the adrenaline spike you experience walking into a hospital ward ebb away or keep you pegged on high alert?

Staying emotionally healthy is a prerequisite for having the focus and energy to attend to others. Being spiritually healthy is even more important—it's what fuels your ability to sense the guidance of the Holy Spirit as you navigate bedside conversations. See the Self-care chapter for suggestions how you can best care for yourself.

- **Debrief the visit with someone in your visitation ministry**

Cover these points: how you feel the visit went, what you feel you did well, where you think you could do better, and what, if any, follow-up you think is needed. You needn't reveal medical details to discover how you might grow in your ability to listen, comfort, and encourage.

- **And, as ever, continue praying**

You may not visit the patient again, but you can continue to pray. Pray for the patient's continued move toward health, physically and spiritually. Pray for the family of the patient as they cope with what's happened to a loved one. And thank God for the honor of serving him in this way.

CHAPTER 8

NURSING HOME VISITS

$\mathcal{K}$erri Loesche has worked in nursing homes for more than twenty years. She's served and loved hundreds of residents and appreciated nearly every visitor who came to see loved ones, friends of friends, or church members.

Why? Because Loesche has seen the good a visit can do. "The loneliness residents deal with is astounding," said Loesche, who noted that some residents she's known had exactly zero visitors over the course of multiple years.

Visiting in a nursing home setting requires the same listening and comforting skills you use elsewhere, but add several special considerations because residents are often elderly and/or in frail health.

When visiting in a nursing home…

Schedule your visit to fit the resident's routines

The elderly are often most alert in the mornings, but that doesn't mean you should arrive at the crack of dawn. Show up after breakfast is over. Mid-afternoon, following lunch and a time of rest, is also often a good time for visits. Call ahead and speak to either the resident or a staff person who serves the resident to ask about timing.

Do a quick sound check

Some residents you visit will probably be hard of hearing. As you initiate a conversation check to see if you can be heard and adjust your volume accordingly. If a television or radio is playing, ask if you can turn it off for the duration of your visit. If outside noise is audible through an open door, ask if you can close the door.

Facing the resident directly helps with not just audio levels, but also by letting the resident see your face and take cues from what they see. Keeping your hand away from your mouth as you speak and enunciating clearly will greatly assist the resident's ability to understand you.

If you're a woman, wearing lipstick can help a hard-of-hearing resident "see" your words as they form. If you're a man, be aware that a significant beard or moustache can hide your words. And if the resident has a "best ear" for hearing, position yourself accordingly.

Take it easy

For many adults, growing older includes growing slower. Everything you've learned about listening and comforting in a hospital setting applies here, too, and may be even more important. But add a generous dollop of patience to the mix.

Residents may pause frequently to search for words or find it hard to complete sentences. Stay engaged and reflect back what was said frequently. It helps elderly residents recall where they were in a narrative.

Share current, relevant information

If you're visiting a church member, bring a recent bulletin and share positive things that are happening in the congregation. Remaining connected with a faith community is often a lifeline for nursing home residents; it reminds them they've not been forgotten: not by the church, and not by God.

Touch—carefully

Appropriate, gentle physical touch can be significant for several reasons. It may be the only touch a resident receives and it's a reminder that you're seeing the resident as a person of value. But only touch if you've been given permission to do so, and limit yourself to placing a reassuring hand on a resident's arm or hand.

That's a caution that Loesche suggests you consider stretching to asking residents if they'd like a hug. "Healthy touch is in short supply," she said, "So if it's okay give hugs. Lots and lots of hugs."

Sooner or later you'll call on a complainer—take it in stride

Some residents resent their living situation. They wish they could live independently, so nothing the facility provides will be quite right. In fact, no matter what the facility delivers, it will be completely wrong.

If a resident is complaining you should listen well and make sure the resident knows his or her concerns have been noted. But don't promise to change anything. If you're hearing the complaints, the facility's staff has probably heard them, too. A quick check with a staff member as you leave will confirm if that's the case.

But pay attention for anything that sounds as if it might be elder abuse or neglect. If you have concerns it's worth checking in with a staff member *after* your visit ends to see if there's something that should be addressed. Don't accuse; there's often a perfectly good explanation for why things are the way they are.

Keep your word

Loesche once worked with a resident whose stroke had left him unable to speak except with a fierce garble.

He was a frustrated, angry man, remembered Loesche: "He couldn't move half his body but he still found a way to hit with his other hand. And it could *hurt*."

Loesche told the resident that she was getting married and promised she'd bring him a piece of wedding cake. From his reaction it was clear he didn't expect she'd come through.

"I showed up with cake while wearing my wedding dress," says Loesche.

"He sat there weeping because I did what I said I'd do."

Loesche's story is a reminder: don't make promises to residents that you can't or won't keep. Empty promises don't bring comfort and they don't honor God.

Select appropriate Scriptures

Some recommendations can be found in Chapter 20, but feel free to shift from those if other passages will more directly meet the needs of the resident. Because you won't know what's appropriate and what isn't, it's often good to put off Scripture reading until later in your visit.

Respect dietary restrictions

"When you come to visit a church member it's fine to bring a small treat of some sort. But respect dietary restrictions," cautions Loesche. "If you're not sure a resident can have those homemade chocolate chip cookies, give them to the kitchen staff to store until they check with the nursing staff."

Remember that residents may have roommates. If the cookies are a problem for a resident's roomie, consider not letting the cookies into the room at all. Don't let your "death by chocolate" brownies become a self-fulfilling prophecy.

Ask where the resident would like to chat

Ambulatory residents may prefer to talk as the two of you take a stroll outside in the sunshine. That preference tells you something about the resident, by the way: it's a clue to ask if the resident was once an avid hiker, gardener, or camper.

Don't assist residents who are looking to exit the building

Loesche said that in some facilities you might encounter two or three residents just inside the door or waiting in the lobby. They want to leave but seem unable to handle the logistics of exiting while in wheelchairs. It's a natural response to want to assist them, but Loesche said that's exactly the wrong thing to do.

"Don't hold the door for any residents leaving the building," she said. "Some residents may be disoriented and want to go home—a home that's no longer there. Helping them leave the facility puts them in danger."

Resident safety is a top-of-the-list concern that plays out in a variety of ways—ways that aren't often understood by visitors.

"Visitors don't always recognize that how the doors operate, how the lobby is set up, how rooms are arranged," said Kerri. "They're the way they are because of safety."

Watch for signs of fatigue

The majority of the visits you make in nursing homes will be with people who are elderly. While older people aren't necessarily less energetic than their younger counterparts, those who live in nursing homes generally are.

If the person you're visiting starts yawning, rubbing her eyes, or otherwise appearing to tire, make your exit. That said, don't necessarily keep your visit to a typical ten or fifteen minutes. If a visit is going well and the resident is energized by the social interaction, when you hit fifteen or twenty minutes ask if the resident feels up to continuing the conversation. You may hear an enthusiastic "yes."

Some of the comfort you're bringing is your simply being there as an attentive listener. Yes, you'll need to get to prayer and sharing Scripture—that's an essential part of why you're there—but it's not the only reason.

73

Let the resident set the pace for your visit.

If you're unsure what to say in this setting, here are some conversation starters:

• Introduce yourself

Explain who you are and that you're representing your church, even if you're calling on a resident who's a long-time church member. The resident may not recognize you in this context or at all, and this will explain why you'll later ask to pray with the resident and also read Scripture passages.

• Comment on the personal items in the resident's room

It's likely you'll see reminders of people and places that are close to the resident's heart. Many residents will have had to significantly downsize their possessions; those you see are the few that made the cut to be kept. Inquire about who and what they represent.

Take note of art. Paintings and framed sketches are fair game for conversation, as is any art taped to the wall or refrigerator door. Ask for more information about what you see and explore how it makes the resident feel.

• Ask about personal and family history

If it's not intrusive, ask about where the resident was born, if the resident has family living in the area, and what the resident's life was like as a child.

•Inquire after the resident's overall health

It's often a front-of-mind topic; let the resident know you're open to hearing what's happening physically. "How are you feeling these days?" is usually enough to prime the pump.

• And there's always the weather and other general topics

Ask how the recent hot/cold/wet/dry weather affects the resident, what activities the resident has been a part of recently, and what's planned for the immediate future. Many nursing homes host card games, group singing, or other programs—see if any are part of the resident's usual routine.

And when a resident has a diagnosis of Alzheimer's...

Following are practical tips for interacting with residents who have a diagnosis of Alzheimer's:

•Speak in short, direct sentences

If possible, include just one idea in each sentence. It will help the person you're visiting follow what you're saying.

• Explain what you'll do before you do it

If you'll be switching off a television, reading a Bible passage, or touching the resident, be sure it's not a surprise.

• Speak slowly and ask one question at a time

It's easier for residents with Alzheimer's to process one thing at a time. Allow the resident time for thinking and forming response.

• But don't talk down to the resident you're visiting

You're visiting an adult. Offer the appropriate deference and respect.

• Don't assume a complete lack of memory

You may talk with a resident and discover she's lucid and able to recall memories perfectly. You may also find that she's unable to recall any of his or her life in the church or even in her family. Be okay with whatever you encounter and be aware it may shift even during your visit.

• Avoid disturbing topics

Whether it's family drama, broken relationships, or financial issues, don't bring up topics that are likely to cause distress. It's exhausting coping with conflict and processing emotion on the best of days and the resident you're visiting may not be having the best day.

•Don't be offended if the resident doesn't recognize you

Your presence can still provide comfort. You are still ministering by providing reassurance and by showing God's love.

CHAPTER 9
IN-HOME VISITS

*J*n-home visits cover a wide range of situations because someone can be homebound for an equally wide range of reasons. People you visit may be recovering from a surgery or illness and have every expectation of soon being back to normal, or may suffer chronic conditions that will leave them homebound forever. They may be elderly adults, adults, teenagers, or even children. They may have been home for just days or for years.

In short, you'll want to gather as much information as possible before making a home visit. Otherwise you could be walking into practically anything.

"I was once told by a church member her neighbor was in deep grief over the loss of a loved one," recalls Lacey. "She was open to a visit so I reached out the next morning. Yes, I should come over—and right away.

"The woman wanted to talk and I was willing to listen," said Lacey. "I asked about her loss and she began sharing what a good friend 'Stretch' had been. Loyal, a great listener, someone she could depend on when she was sad or depressed.

"We were a good ten minutes into the visit before I realized she was talking about a *pet* who'd died, not a person. And not just any pet—a *boa constrictor*." At first Lacey thought her friend was pranking her, but the woman she was visiting seemed genuinely distressed. So Lacey soldiered on and discovered that "Stretch" may have been a snake but he was also a beloved companion. And the neighbor was truly grieving.

"All in all it was a good visit," said Lacey. "But I did tell my friend she should have tipped me off about 'Stretch.'"

Lacey's respect for the woman's pain allowed Lacey to be helpful. Her commitment to listening well and comforting others let her be effective. She suspended judgment and made a difference. The essential skills you use in every visit will make you equally helpful in home visits, but there are some special considerations you should keep in mind.

Homebound doesn't equal helpless

If you're visiting a member of your church who's homebound long term, that person still has gifts to share with your church.

One visitor remembers calling on a woman who was formerly a small group leader in their congregation. "I felt guilty when I left because it always seemed I got more than I gave. Helen asked about my family, prayed about what was going on in my life, and suggested relevant Scripture I might read. It was great." After Helen was no longer able to get to church she asked if she could write to the congregation's missionaries to provide encouragement. When her failing vision made that impossible, she got lists of other homebound members and phoned them frequently to check up on them.

"And when she could no longer do that she asked for the names of church members who were ill so she could pray for them," Helen may have been homebound, but she was a spiritual warrior.

The moral of this story: if appropriate, you might ask if the person you're visiting has the energy and interest to continue serving as part of a prayer chain, making calls to encourage others, or meeting with someone for mentoring. But make whatever service opportunity you offer real: it has to have significance and come with deadlines, training, and accountability.

Homebound visits can be frequent

Mike gets together with John every month.

"I initially visited him in the hospital when he was hospitalized with brain cancer," said Mike. "Everyone expected John to die within a week, but he recovered enough to go home—where I've been visiting him for several years."

The tumors that dot John's scans still remain and he knows he could spiral downward at any time. His health is frail, but his mind remains sharp. "His condition prompts John to do some deep thinking and consider spiritual things with a refreshing honesty," said Mike. "We've become friends. I look forward to our times together."

You may form an ongoing friendship, too. And for many homebound people your visits will become highlights on their calendars. "I appreciate the visits," said John. "I like knowing someone out there remembers and values me."

To a homebound person relationships may be everything. They feel imprisoned, cut off, abandoned. Occasional follow-up visits or phone calls are like oxygen.

Don't forget the caregivers

John's wife, Shelly, has found herself nearly as homebound as John because of the care he needs, so Mike is careful to encourage her, too. Unpaid, non-professional caregivers find their lives overwhelmed by an avalanche of medical visits, insurance paperwork, bedpan duty, and the draining demands of an illness that has invaded their home.

They're looking for respite, an hour or two away from their duties so they can rest and relax. Your visits, if they're scheduled at the right times, can provide that as you sit with the person you're visiting. That won't be the case the first time you visit, but should you make visiting a homebound patient a regular thing, you may be blessing two people when you go.

Consider doing in-home visits in pairs

You're entering the home of someone who's vulnerable, so it's important you stay above reproach. Conduct yourself with caution so nobody can accuse you of any wrong or exploitive behavior.

A simple way to avoid any misunderstandings and protect yourself from accusations is to take someone with you, or to call only on homebound people of your gender.

"The downside of joint visits is that it's unlikely the three of you will become friends," said Mike. "John and I have a lot of interests in common so our friendship grew naturally. I'm not sure that would have happened had I visited with someone else every time."

If your visitation ministry has a policy, follow it. If there's no policy, talk about this issue and come to a resolution. And if you'll be visiting children or teenagers at home, connect with the directors of your children's and youth ministries. They're your in-house experts as to what's appropriate and inappropriate when visiting young people.

You can expect to hear that an adult is never alone with a child, and that parents need to be apprised of serious conversations. You may also be cautioned to use age-appropriate language when dealing with young children.

Also, here's a reminder: when you're visiting a young child, you're also visiting that child's parents. Always reserve enough time that you can check in with the parents, too. How are they doing? What do they need?

Pray for the child, pray for the parents. Comfort the child, comfort the parents.

CHAPTER 10

IN-HOME VISITS WITH THE HEALTHY

*T*here was a time filling out a church's visitor card guaranteed a knock on your door. Standing on the porch would be several smiling church members, Bibles in hand, dropping by to offer a warm handshake and an invitation to the next church potluck.

Back then, drop-in visits were considered neighborly. Now they're just as likely to be viewed as stalking. "We no longer do in-person visits," said Ed, talking about how his Colorado church follows up with visitors.

Ed, for one, misses those visits. "They were a way to connect," he said, "a way to help visitors feel special. But fewer and fewer people were home, or welcomed a visit. We had to find other ways to reach out."

If your visitation team calls on church visitors as well as the sick, you'll need to decide whether you'll send teams to make in-person visits, or find other ways to invite visitors to come back.

Until you gather contact information from visitors you won't be doing anything. And people have never been more cautious about handing out personal information. So make it safe for visitors to tell you who they are and how to reach them. Tell them *why* you're asking to get in touch so they can decide how much information to give you.

Explain you'd like to tell them more about the church and promise you won't flood them with unwanted emails and calls. That's usually enough to prompt a name and email address, perhaps even a physical address and phone number.

Here are three ways to collect that data:

• Pew cards still come in handy

Design your own and label them "Connection Cards." Ask for contact information and also include boxes to check if the person filling out the card would like prayer, to hear from a pastor, or would like to know more about the church.

When someone fills in an address and request for information, that's permission to make a visit.

• Check with the children's ministry area

Parents provide basic contact information as a matter of course when signing in their kids. Use it to get back in touch with the parents to thank them for their kids' attendance. Just be sure you collect information *only* from parents; never quiz kids on where they live or their contact information.

• Staff an information booth

Mention in the worship service you have a small gift for visitors and that you'd appreciate their stopping by the booth. Some churches have a loaf of fresh bread waiting and others have a $5.00 gift card to a local coffee shop.

Ed's church has built their information booth smack in the middle of the lobby, just outside the sanctuary. Ed and his crew do more than sit in the booth waiting for visitors to find them. They stand *outside* the booth, eyes up, scanning the crowd, engaging visitors in conversation as visitors pass by.

"We do that first visit before people leave our building," he said. They introduce themselves, hand visitors an information packet, and suggest church programming that might be especially relevant to each visitor.

"We also ask for contact information so we can check back during the week to hear what the visitors thought of their experience," said Ed. "We tell visitors their opinions will be helpful and most people are happy to help out."

If at all possible, that second conversation happens at the home of the visitors.

If you make an at-home visit, here are things to keep in mind:

• Move fast

Peoples' attention spans are short. If someone visits you on Sunday, plan to return the favor within 72 hours. Saying you're glad someone came rings hollow when it takes two or three weeks to say it.

• Consider scheduling

If you've captured a visitor's phone number, call to ask if it's okay to stop by for five minutes and arrange a time. Be clear you won't be staying; you're just coming by to say "thanks" or hear what the visitor thought of your church, and to drop off a small gift.

Or take your chances and just show up—it's your call.

• Keep it short and sweet

Five minutes means five minutes. If you're invited in for a longer conversation, great. But let that be the choice of the people you visit: at the five-minute mark be ready to leave. Think it can't be done? Here was Ed's front-door speech back when he was making at-home visits:

Hello—my name is Ed and I'm from First Christian Church. We just stopped by to thank you for visiting us last Sunday. I brought you a bit more information about who we are, what we do, and what might be of interest to you and your family.
(Hands over a thin information packet)

And I brought you this little gift, too. (Hands over a $5 Starbucks card)
Enjoy a cup of coffee on us this week. And if you have questions about anything in the packet give me a call—my name and number is on the card—and maybe we can have that cup of coffee together so I can answer your questions.
So thanks again for coming—and I hope we'll see you again. If you have just a minute, is there anything you'd like to know right now?

That's everything you need to say in 45 seconds. Inviting, personal, zero pressure, and easy to say with a smile.

• Come bearing gifts

It can be practically anything, but Starbucks cards seem to always work well. One wonders what visitors carried before Starbucks colonized the continent!

• Leave with expectation

You're inviting the visitor to return but even more, you're initiating a relationship. Express hope you'll see visitor again and then *watch for that visitor* on coming Sundays. Be ready to greet the person by name if the visitor returns.

• And always be ready to present the Gospel

The Lord may have brought a visitor to your church because that person is dealing with issues that have opened his or her heart to the Gospel. If you're seeing or hearing anything that might indicate a readiness to address a problem or receive Christ, kick your listening and caring into high gear and engage at that level.

A sample prayer to lead when someone is receiving Jesus is in Chapter 21.

And if you'll follow up without making visits, here are some suggestions…

Pay extra attention to your information booth

Take a leaf from Ed's playbook and put the information booth where it can't be avoided. When you're staffing the booth, don't chat with your friends. Instead, be on the lookout for people you don't know.

Prepare to be embarrassed when you try to hand an information packet to someone who's been attending for 18 years. If you're in a large church, it'll happen but that's okay.

You'll remember those people forever.

If you follow up with a telephone call, quickly identify yourself

Share your name and the name of your church right up front. State quickly why you're calling and invite a return call. Plan on leaving a message, by the way: many people won't pick up a call from a number they don't already know.

And you did call at a reasonable hour, yes? No early morning or midnight calls!

Craft emails that can be easily adapted

Never send a "Dear Visitor" standardized email. Write something that allows you to drop in a reference to the sermon topic, an upcoming church event, anything that communicates this is a person-to-person communication, not a form letter.

Use a "drip campaign"

Marketers know there's value in strategically making contact multiple times at key moments. Like the steady drip of a leaky faucet, those touches increase the likelihood you'll be remembered and heard. Don't let your visits be "one and done," giving visitors one shot at asking questions or connecting with you.

Email and texts are excellent ways to stay in contact—with four cautions.

First, always have a way to easily opt out of additional contacts. That reassures message recipients they're in control of how much access they want to give you.

Second, always have something to say. Briefly mention an upcoming program, a service opportunity, or a new small group open for members.

Third, always link to your church website. That's where message recipients can go to get details.

Finally, keep it to one contact per week, if that. Sending more emails doesn't increase your impact; less is more.

Consider sending a letter to adults. Always send letters to children

Few people send actual stamp-on-envelope letters any longer, so they make a big impression. Hand address the envelope, use stamps rather than a postage meter, and send your "thanks for visiting, hope to see you soon" letter no later than Monday afternoon so it arrives by midweek.

Because kids love getting letters and seldom do, follow up with them by mail. Include a puzzle page, a small game, or another surprise—they'll be enthused about returning to visit again. Good news: they'll probably bring their parents with them!

CHAPTER 11

MEDICAL REHABILITATION FACILITY VISITS

*F*irst, a qualifier: in this chapter we're looking at you visiting a medical facility, *not* one that specializes in dealing with addictions. That's a separate environment and will be addressed in a different chapter.

Skilled nursing or short-term rehab medical facilities are environments where people can regain strength and daily living skills following surgery, illness, or another medical episode. They're where patients work with physical, occupational, and/or speech therapists as well as receiving ongoing medical care.

Some of the patients you'll be asked to visit will be in a facility like this after they're discharged from a hospital but before they make their way home. When visiting an in-patient rehab facility, you'll apply all the skills and tips discussed in Chapter 7 (Hospital Visits)—plus factor in these specific concerns:

• **In rehab facilities patients are often out of their rooms**

In a hospital you have a good chance of catching a patient in his or her room. It's just the opposite in a rehab facility as patients experience days filled with one location-based therapy after another.

Rather than recuperating in bed they're in an exercise room doing activities tailored to help them regain their ability to balance, handle stairs, or other specific goals. Or they may be in a kitchen setting remastering the ability to prepare meals. Or a therapy pool working on rebuilding muscle mass after weeks in bed.

In an age of cell phones and in-room phone extensions, it's usually possible to reach a patient to arrange an appointment. Do that to increase your odds of making a successful call.

• Patients are often exhausted after a day of therapy

Another reason to arrange an appointment is because therapy is *hard work*.

Tricia, whose Guillain-Barre disease robbed her of many motor skills, was in a therapy setting for a month and remembers how just walking across a room left her so tired she was in tears.

"Therapy pushes you to do just a bit more than what you can do," she remembers. "That means at the end of the day, when the therapies are over, you've used up whatever reserve of energy you had and then some. You're looking forward to bed, not visitors."

Mornings in rehab facilities usually are given to breakfast, taking care of bathing, dressing, and grooming—which could require help—and the medical staff completing their rounds. Then it's straight to therapy appointments until lunch, followed by additional sessions before dinner.

There are usually narrow windows of time that a patient will be available and able to visit. Asking when those windows are—and being careful to not overstay your welcome—is key when making visits in these facilities.

• Patients won't be there as long as you think

Don't be lulled into putting off your visit thinking the patient will be in the facility for months. The average length of stay is about two weeks and that factors in strokes, traumatic brain injuries, and other extended stays.

Someone recovering from surgery may find themselves headed home after just a few days.

- **There's a strong focus on what life will be like after leaving**

In a hospital a serious illness may have patients wondering if they'll live or die. In a rehab facility that issue has probably been resolved: they know they'll live—but they're wondering what that life will be like.

Which means you may find yourself dealing with significant anger and disappointment: with life, with God, with themselves, with family and friends. These patients are facing limitations they never expected to face and coping with challenges that may feel overwhelming.

Plus, now that they're on a pathway to recovery, the outpouring of support they received in the hospital may be evaporating. They may feel forgotten or abandoned.

Don't be put off if you come to share what's positive in life and faith and you meet a wall of negative emotion. If that's what a patient is feeling, it's what that patient is feeling. Listen, care, and don't judge.

- **Consider checking back with an additional visit or two**

A patient in rehab has entered a marathon, and there's a reason at many marathons cheering people hand out cups of water at regular intervals. Encouragement fades fast, and a regular diet of support can be the boost a patient needs to go the distance.

Ask if you can call back (either in person or on the phone) in a day or two to see how things are progressing. If you get a "yes" don't pull out of the parking lot without putting an alarm on your phone as a reminder.

Again: never make a promise you can't or won't keep.

CHAPTER 12

ADDICTION REHABILITATION FACILITY AND PSYCHIATRIC UNIT VISITS

First, know this: you may not be able to visit at all, at least at the beginning of someone's stay.

Some facilities permit just immediate family members to visit and others will accommodate friends and well wishers, but only during very limited hours. The rules shift from facility to facility, so call ahead or check the facility's website.

There's a good rationale for limiting visits to people in rehab. It may be that a break from the "outside" world is needed to move therapy ahead, or that it's all a person can do to focus on healing and building relationships within the facility. An outside person, especially one who's not a trained therapist, may create confusion or turmoil.

So check—and then double-check. If the patient shares with therapists that you or your church are a positive support in his or her life you may find you're welcome.

If you can't make a personal visit, ask about sending a letter or email. Be flexible about how you make contact.

If you do go, expect to accommodate some requests

You may be asked to leave personal belongings in your vehicle or with staff members. You may have to sign in and out, and to provide identification. You may be searched to assure you're not carrying drugs or alcohol.

Don't be offended, the staff is guaranteeing the safety of the person you're visiting. You're not being singled out for any reason; if searching visitors is a policy it's being applied to everyone who parks in the visitors' lot.

Be encouraging and supportive

Some people, including those who end up in rehab, view addictions as personal moral failure. If that's your take on alcoholism or opioid addiction, have another visitor make the call.

It's hard being in rehab, to face something that feels too big to tame. Just being in rehab itself may be creating tensions whether financial, professional, or family. Don't pile on. Instead, encourage and support. Your body language, your smile, and your listening without judgment will all say, "I'm here to help. And so is Jesus."

Ask how the person is doing, but don't push

Some people in rehab don't want to discuss their treatment any more than a hospital patient may wish to reveal medical details.

Apply the same guidelines about listening here as in the hospital. You're not there to do therapy; you're there to bring light and life.

Be careful about focusing on the future

It's very possible an inpatient is learning how to be fully in the present and less concerned about the past and future. Managing addiction is a moment-by-moment thing; you firing off questions about what the person will do after checking out of the facility may be overwhelming.

If you let the patient lead the conversation, you'll avoid stepping on this land mine.

Consider being a regular visitor

Unlike patients in a hospital, someone admitted to rehab may spend weeks in a facility. A supportive visitor becomes a treat, and you'll find that inpatients look forward to your arrival.

Be especially careful to be on time if you've scheduled an appointment. You may have a narrow window of time allowed for you to be with the inpatient. Your punctuality also signals that the visit and the inpatient are important to you.

CHAPTER 13

EMERGENCY ROOM VISITS

$\mathcal{A}$ call comes in that a congregation member is in the emergency room. Can you come at once? Typically, these requests reach you after the patient has cycled through the ER and been admitted, discharged, or rushed into emergency treatment. If you see anyone in the ER, it's likely to be the family of the patient.

If that's where you find yourself, here are some tips:

Promptly identify yourself and explain why you're there

A church member's family may not know you or your church. Put the family at ease by making it clear who you are and why you're there. Don't assume that they're the ones who called for you, or that they were expecting you to come.

Respect family dynamics

There's a lot you don't know. Are an injured child's parents—both of whom are there—divorced or married? Is there blame being passed around for whatever happened? Don't make assumptions. Without judging, observe what you can and then move ahead carefully.

Be brief

Ask about the situation and then ask if you can invite God into the situation with a brief prayer. Don't assume anyone will pray with you as you pray aloud, but make the offer.

Ask if you should linger or leave

More family or friends may be arriving momentarily. A medical consult may be just around the corner. There may be family matters to discuss without you.

If the patient is being treated or in surgery, offer to sit with the family members awhile if they'd like you to join them. Or offer to fetch coffee or make a phone call or two on behalf of the family.

Whether you're asked to linger or leave, leave your name and phone number behind in case the family—or the patient—wishes to be in touch.

CHAPTER 14

VISITING THE ELDERLY

*A*ge isn't an illness, but you may be called to visit with a congregation member who is generally healthy, just elderly. See the Nursing Home chapter for general recommendations, but keep reading if you're wondering what you might do or say during your visit.

Read aloud

Fading vision may make reading difficult for an elderly person and there's comfort in hearing another human voice. Ask if there's a section of scripture that's especially meaningful.

Import some humor

You'll find clean, easy-to-understand stories and jokes in magazines like the *Reader's Digest*, and inspiration in many of the *Chicken Soup for the Soul* series of books.

Some specific suggestions are noted in the Resources section.

Offer to look through photo albums

Your life may be archived digitally, but some elderly people still have photo albums. Ask to see them and you'll get a guided tour of the person's life. Be curious. Ask questions not just about history but the person's faith journey, too.

Ask for stories

Stories about time in school. Who their childhood friends were. What sports they played, what hobbies they enjoyed, what their parents did for work. And, if they're widowed, ask about their spouses: elderly widows are seldom asked about that important person in their lives.

Affirm significance

Roles and activities that gave elderly peoples' lives meaning may have disappeared. Children are grown and gone, careers over. Elderly people may wonder why it's worth getting up in the morning.

Remind them who they are in Christ, and that their calling to worship, serve, pray, and grow spiritually hasn't ended. They're preparing for an eternity in heaven in part by being involved in the lives of the people they're with now.

Offer small assistance

It's small in that you can't turn back the clock or restore a beloved spouse who has died. But you can change a light bulb that's gone out in a hallway or pick up a stack of books that's fallen to the floor.

Both high and low tasks may be beyond the elderly person you're visiting. If you see something obvious, offer to help.

Reassure and comfort

Pick passages to read and a prayer to share that's warm and comforting. Those you visit may have experienced loss after loss; remind them of what they've gained as believers.

CHAPTER 15

VISITING THE TERMINALLY ILL

*W*hen visiting those who are near death, add this to the listening and compassion you bring with you: A willingness to embrace silence. Your presence may be all the person needs or wants. It may be all she can handle and is comfort enough.

Keep the following considerations in mind as you plan your visit, too:

Stay tightly focused on the person you're visiting

What's happening in your life pales by comparison to what she's hearing and seeing. Keep the focus on her, kindly and gently redirecting the conversation to what she's thinking, feeling, and experiencing. It's okay to be more directional if the person is nearing death.

If the person is terminally ill but death isn't imminent, do what you normally do and let her take the lead in conversation.

Bring a Bible and use it

Your words are nice, but God's words are powerful. Be sure they're heard.

Offer touch

With the person's permission, hold her hand. Or place her hand on yours so if she chooses to break off contact it's easy to do so.

Keep any conversation positive

You may hear about regrets, or sadness that she won't live to hold a new grandchild or repair a relationship. Don't argue, but do remind her that God is still at work and can finish what she leaves undone.

Honor the person's legacy and impact

If she's blessed you or others, if she's raised a family, if she's served God in some way, remind her. You're bringing dignity to someone who may have had it stripped away by incontinence and fear.

God called the person you see before you to a life of purpose. Let her know that you appreciate what she did to say "yes" to God. Be generous.

If you ask questions, make them direct

Avoid Christian jargon like, "How are you finding victory in this?" or "What's the Lord teaching you?" Those are hard to decode. Instead, ask "How are you feeling today?" or "What's hard right now?" The terminally ill are preoccupied; don't clutter your communication.

Invite words of advice

Not necessarily about anything in particular, but in general. Ask if there's something the person wishes to say to you or the world. Listen carefully: those who are dying often distill their identities and beliefs into a few precious lines.

Ooze peace

Through your tone of voice, your affect, and your gentleness, send a message of comforting peace. This isn't a time to correct theological nuance or challenge attitudes.

CHAPTER 16

VISITING SOMEONE IN QUARANTINE

*A*nyone in quarantine (in a hospital, at home, in prison, anywhere) is there for a reason, and your physical visit may put that person—or you—at risk. Yet they're exactly the people who may be most in need of care, comfort, and a reminder they've not been forgotten by God or their church family. But what can you do when someone you feel called to visit is isolated? When their physical condition makes a visit inadvisable…or impossible?

Check with the chaplain

If the person you wish to visit is in a hospital or a care facility that has a chaplains' office, call it. If anyone will get permission to enter a patient's room, it's likely to be a chaplain familiar with the medical staff and with access to the necessary equipment to visit safely.

Asking a chaplain to carry your message of encouragement to the person you wish to visit is always an option. The individual you wish to serve may not get *your* visit, but he or she will receive *a* visit—and that's a plus. The chaplain may also be able to deliver a note or small gift you sent to the chaplain prior to the visit.

Write a letter, send a card

In some situations, paper that's been sterilized can go where people aren't allowed. Call to find out if that's possible and, if so, write what you have to say. Be positive and upbeat, but honestly share what's on your heart. This is a time-honored way to visit, by the way: nearly half of the New Testament is comprised of letters sent to believers who couldn't be visited because of distance.

Tap technology

People in quarantine may or may not have access to a cell phone or tablet so you'll need to ask. If there's access to technology and an ability to use it, you can visit virtually through text, email, or videotelephony.

The facility where the person you wish to visit is staying will be able to tell you about policies concerning access to technology. A family member will be able to tell you about a person's ability to use technology. If someone's unable to access or use technology, see if that family member is able to carry in a screen to show the brief videotaped greeting you've forwarded to the family member.

And then there's this...

Some creative ways to encourage without contact have emerged that are worth a mention, too. During the coronavirus pandemic it became routine for visits to happen through closed windows, a grandparent or friend standing outside a home while a quarantined child looked on from a few feet away.

There were drive-by birthday parties, graduations, and even funerals. Supportive signs held up from nearby sidewalks. Messages of love spelled out by stamping letters in the snow. What's a creative way you can encourage someone who's feeling forgotten? A way to communicate care and to usher God's grace into someone's life?

CHAPTER 17

REQUESTING A VISIT

*M*any care and visitation ministries miss opportunities to visit because there's no quick, easy way for someone to notify the church that a visit is desired.

Typically someone calls the church office and leaves a message that's either picked up by a staff member or the pastor the following day...maybe. Another day is lost connecting with the ministry coordinator who then has to connect with you so you can make a visit.

No wonder that at times, when you arrive at a hospital room, a patient or family member wonders where you've been. You may have dropped everything to get there, but the initial call may have been made days earlier.

If that's what you encounter, be understanding by saying, "I'm sorry nobody came sooner but I just found out about your situation a few hours ago and I'm here now. How are you feeling?"

Don't be defensive. Don't explain the complications of phone tag. Just apologize and move on to the purpose of your visit: to listen, to pray, to invite God's grace into the room. But if this *does* happen, make a mental note to bring it up at the next visitation team meeting and brainstorm some ways to speed up and simplify communication.

Here are some options, by the way:

Provide the visitation ministry coordinator's mobile number?

In the church bulletin, in the newsletter, on the voice mail system, everywhere: list the visitation ministry coordinator's personal mobile number.

If that sounds like a good idea, that's probably because you're not the coordinator.

While it's an efficient system—one phone call gets someone in crisis straight to the person who can arrange a visit—it means somebody's on call 24/7/365. That's a sizable commitment and means your coordinator won't be able to screen unknown numbers, has to check messages and texts frequently, and needs to arrange back-up to allow for vacations and days away from a phone.

Don't go this route. You'll pull the plug on the idea in a month or two and then have to walk back the offer to be instantly available.

Dedicate a church voice mailbox for visitation requests

For most voice mail systems it's as easy as adding an option along these lines: "If you or a loved one has experienced a medical emergency and you'd like someone from the church to visit, please press '7.'"

Once a caller is in the correct box, continue: "Please provide the following information: your name, a phone number where we can reach you, and the name and location of the person you'd like us to visit. Repeat the information twice, slowly and clearly. Please note we may need to contact you for additional information before making the visit. Thank you."

That's a lot of message, but you need it all to avoid barging into someone's hospital room uninvited.

Ask for the information twice. People may be calling while stressed or from a busy (and noisy) emergency room, where it's easy for a message to become garbled.

Churches using this system will need to provide passwords to whoever is on call from the visitation ministry so the visitor can check for messages daily. Or, if passing out passwords isn't tenable, someone on church staff will need to make it a priority to check for calls at least once per day.

Consider adding digital

Sue Blagg has served for 15 years as the Saddleback Church Lake Forest campus contact person for hospital visitation. Phone the church office to ask that you or someone you know receive a visit while hospitalized, and she's on the other end of that call.

Though she knows that many—if not most—of the hospital calls made by church members never come to her attention.

"Saddleback is a church of small groups," said Sue. "When someone in a small group ends up in the hospital it's often their small group members who visit and care for that person."

But if for some reason that doesn't happen, church members are invited to fill out a Hospital Visitation Request at the church website. They can request a visit for themselves, their friends, or their neighbors, so long as whoever is to be visited has requested the visit.

When a form is submitted, Sue contacts a hospital team volunteer and passes along the relevant information: who's hospitalized, where they're staying, when they expect to be released, and basic facts about the patient. Also included: who's making the request, what's known about why the person is hospitalized, and that all-important confirmation that the patient will welcome the visit.

Having an online way for congregants to reach out to the Saddleback hospital team opens an additional way to trigger a visit and lets team leaders not be perpetually waiting by the phone. If your church has a website that's able to collect confidential information, it's relatively easy to set up your own system.

But because there are situations that require immediate voice-to-voice connection, Sue has a phone contact listed at the team's website—just in case.

"Our website doesn't lead to all that many visits," said Sue. "We hear about visits we can make mostly by word of mouth. But when a form's submitted, we follow up."

Like all situations where information is submitted electronically, the efficiency of this system is only as good as the diligence with information is checked.

Or there's this: Rely on whatever's working now

If you're a church of 100 members, relying on messages left in the church office may be enough. People know each other. They know how to reach out the pastor directly if the situation is serious.

If no balls are being dropped, don't worry about fixing what's not broken.

But be aware: *you're* the one who'll know if there's a problem. If you're hearing that there's a significant gap between when visits are requested and when you're getting to the hospital, that's your permission to raise a question about process.

CHAPTER 18

HIPAA AND YOU

$\mathcal{G}$ enerally speaking, HIPAA (Health and Insurance Portability and Accountability Act) Privacy Rules don't apply to a church's disclosure of health-related information, at least in the context of prayer lists.[2]

That's especially true if the list isn't printed or widely distributed and instead exists on a portion of the church website that requires a login to access. But that said, if you were a patient who received a visit, how much detail about your medical condition would you want revealed to someone else? Everyone else? That you're ill and would appreciate prayer? That you're ill, at St. Francis Hospital, and you'd appreciate prayer? Or that you're ill courtesy of a vasectomy that went poorly and caused an infection, and that you're at St. Francis Hospital and would appreciate prayer? You get the point.

Though sharing a bit of information may be legal, it's possible it will also be viewed as an invasion of privacy, and that can feel like personal betrayal. It certainly won't bring comfort, and medical details aren't necessary when praying.

So when you're visiting, do this:

---

2 https://www.brotherhoodmutual.com/resources/safety-library/risk-management-articles/administrative-staff-and-finance/some-not-all-ministries-are-subject-to-hipaa-requirements

Ask if the patient wants to be added to a prayer list

Be clear what information will accompany the patient's name. If you don't receive a verbal confirmation, don't place the person's name on the list.

Keep medical information general, not specific

"Kimberly Harris is recovering from an illness" is enough to prompt prayer. You needn't go into specifics. Neither should you disclose any emotional information you encounter as you actively listen during the visit.

If you provide a written summary of your visit, do so carefully

Don't cover specific medical situations even in an email to your visitation team members. Don't discuss treatments, report on prognosis, or share your opinions as to medical outcomes. Simply provide the who, what, when, and where of the visit—the facts and the facts only. Be sure your facts aren't the medical facts.

If it's a church employee being visited, be especially diligent

It's one thing to release information about a member of your congregation, but HIPAA laws are more rigorous about what employers can and can't release about employees like a pastor, church secretary, or church custodian.

For many churches, HIPAA isn't a legal concern, it's an ethical one. That you can't be sued for revealing sensitive medical information doesn't mean it's caring or kind to share it with others.

Plus, if you or your fellow visitors gain a reputation for being gossips, you can safely assume that few visits will be requested even if a patient is desperate for comfort and prayer.

CHAPTER 19

MAKING A REFERRAL

*A*s you're talking to patients you may become aware of very real needs in their lives.

They're worried about finances, how to afford the care they're now receiving or will require when they return to a home that suddenly needs a wheelchair ramp and grab bars.

They may wonder about how they'll continue caring for a beloved pet, who will help them with toileting, or how to go about selecting a rehab facility. An illness can destroy in a moment the routines that have taken a lifetime to put in place.

"For some patients an episode can draw a hard 'before and after' line in their lives," said Doctor Tom. "Before the stroke they were independent, now they have to rely on others. Before the cancer they were those people who were always out and about and now a big day is getting from the bedroom to the living room.

"They've lost that former life and have to figure out how to make the new one work."

As you sit at the bedside of a person whose needs are overwhelming, your empathy may tempt you to try to meet those needs yourself. Doing so wouldn't be wrong; it's part of the call on a believer's life to be the Samaritan who tends to the wounds of strangers.

But what do you really have the capacity to do—and keep doing? Will you make daily visits to the person's home to take care of that aging dog? Install hardware throughout the house to make it work for someone whose balance has disappeared? One thing you *can* do is to make a referral to organizations that are able to provide specific types of help. But to do that, you need to know who they are and how to contact them.

Here are some tips for having referrals ready.

Start where you are. Who at the hospital can be a resource?

Depending on the situation and the hospital, before a patient is discharged a case manager or social worker may step in to determine what the patient requires once he or she gets home. This person will be networked with community resources already set up to meet the patient's needs.

Let the patient find out first what's available off this help menu and then consider what else your church might do.

Know about any service teams that exist within your church

If there are small groups or ministries that specialize in building code-compliant wheelchair ramps, reach out to them now so you know what they can and can't do, and on what timeline.

If there's a ministry that takes meals to a family that's experienced illness or loss, have that contact information and know their boundaries regarding who they serve and for how long. The ministry may be for church members only, or more widely available to friends and family of church members. Check with your church office for that information and carry it with you when you make a visit.

Decide now if you'll do follow-up visits

Some visitation ministries visit once, and that's it. Others encourage visitors to connect with a patient at least once more after the patient is home.

If your ministry has a policy, follow it. If there's no policy, prayerfully decide what your personal boundaries are.

Continue praying

You can pray for the patient you visit but be cautious about making a referral regarding prayer. Some churches publish lists of prayer concerns in their Sunday bulletins or online. Before you add a patient's name to that list get permission to do so from the patient.

Assuming you've gotten permission, don't reveal any medical information along with the name. Even listing the hospital can imply that the patient is eager to see a flood of visitors—and that may not be the case.

CHAPTER 20

BIBLE PASSAGES TO COMFORT
AND ENCOURAGE

Anxiety and worry
"Cast all your anxiety on him because he cares for you."
(1 Peter 5:7)

Also: 2 Timothy 1:7, Isaiah 41:10, Philippians 4:6-7, Matthew
6:25-34

Bitterness
*"...so that Christ may dwell in your hearts through faith.
And I pray that you, being rooted and established in love,
may have power, together with all the Lord's holy people, to
grasp how wide and long and high and deep is the love of
Christ, and to know this love that surpasses knowledge—that
you may be filled to the measure of all the fullness of God."*
(Ephesians 3:17-19)

Also: Psalm 51:10; Ephesians 4:26; Proverbs 14:10

Comfort
*"May your unfailing love be my comfort, according to your
promise to your servant."* (Psalm 119:76)

Also: Psalm 103:1-14, 2 Corinthians 1:3-5, Psalm 27:1; Psalm
94:19; Hebrews 4:14-16

Confusion

> *"Let the morning bring me word of your unfailing love, for I have put my trust in you. Show me the way I should go, for to you I entrust my life."* (Psalm 143:8)

Also: 1 Corinthians 14:33; 2 Timothy 1:7

Discouragement

> *"For our light and momentary troubles are achieving for us an eternal glory that far outweighs them all. So we fix our eyes not on what is seen, but on what is unseen, since what is seen is temporary, but what is unseen is eternal."* (2 Corinthians 4:17-18)

Also: Proverbs 3:5-6; Psalm 31:24; Psalm 55:22

Eternal life with Jesus

> *"Do not let your hearts be troubled. You believe in God; believe also in me. My Father's house has many rooms; if that were not so, would I have told you that I am going there to prepare a place for you? And if I go and prepare a place for you, I will come back and take you to be with me that you also may be where I am."* (John 14:1-3)

Also: John 10:27-30; 1 Peter 1:3-5; Philippians 1:21-23

Fearful

> *"The Lord is my light and my salvation—whom shall I fear? The Lord is the stronghold of my life—of whom shall I be afraid?"* (Psalm 27:1)

Also: 1 Peter 5:6-7, Psalm 34:4; Psalm 56:3

Feeling weary and overwhelmed

> *"Come to me, all you who are weary and burdened, and I will give you rest. Take my yoke upon you and learn from*

me, for I am gentle and humble in heart, and you will find rest for your souls. For my yoke is easy and my burden is light." (Matthew 11:28-30)

Also: Romans 8:28; James 1:12; Hebrews 12:1-3; Psalm 61:1-4

Gospel

"You see, at just the right time, when we were still powerless, Christ died for the ungodly. Very rarely will anyone die for a righteous person, though for a good person someone might possibly dare to die. But God demonstrates his own love for us in this: While we were still sinners, Christ died for us. Since we have now been justified by his blood, how much more shall we be saved from God's wrath through him! For if, while we were God's enemies, we were reconciled to him through the death of his Son, how much more, having been reconciled, shall we be saved through his life! Not only is this so, but we also boast in God through our Lord Jesus Christ, through whom we have now received reconciliation."

(Romans 5:6-11)

Also: John 11:25-26; Ephesians 2:1-10; John 3:16

Grieving

"May the God of hope fill you with all joy and peace as you trust in him, so that you may overflow with hope by the power of the Holy Spirit." (Romans 15:13)

Also: Revelation 21:4; Psalm 34:18, Matthew 5:4; Luke 6:21

Helplessness

"But as for me, I am poor and needy; may the Lord think of me. You are my help and my deliverer; you are my God, do not delay." (Psalm 40:17)

Also: Psalm 42:5; Psalm 33:20; Psalm 10:12

Hopelessness

"God is our refuge and strength, an ever-present help in trouble. Therefore we will not fear, though the earth give way and the mountains fall into the heart of the sea, though its waters roar and foam and the mountains quake with their surging." (Psalm 46:1-3)

Also: Proverbs 18:10; Nehemiah 8:10; Psalm 32:7-8; Psalm 62:5-6; Psalm 42:5

Impending death

"But our citizenship is in heaven. And we eagerly await a Savior from there, the Lord Jesus Christ, who, by the power that enables him to bring everything under his control, will transform our lowly bodies so that they will be like his glorious body." (Philippians 3:20-21)

Also: Revelation 21:4; John 5:24; John 11:25; Psalm 27:1; John 11:25-26; Isaiah 25:8, Romans 14:8

Loneliness

"Who shall separate us from the love of Christ? Shall trouble or hardship or persecution or famine or nakedness or danger or sword?... No, in all these things we are more than conquerors through him who loved us. For I am convinced that neither death nor life, neither angels nor demons, neither the present nor the future, nor any powers, neither height nor depth, nor anything else in all creation, will be able to separate us from the love of God that is in Christ Jesus our Lord." (Romans 8:35, 37-39)

Also: Matthew 28:20; Psalm 25:16-21, Luke 12:6-7

Old age

"Even when I am old and gray, do not forsake me, my God, till I declare your power to the next generation, your mighty acts to all who are to come." (Psalm 71:18)

Also: Isaiah 46: 4; Psalm 143:5

Pain and suffering

"I have told these things, so that in me you may have peace. In this world you will have trouble. But take heart! I have overcome the world." (John 16:33)

Also: Romans 12:12; James 1:2-4; 1 Peter 5:10. Romans 8:18

Peace

"I have told you these things, so that in me you may have peace. In this world you will have trouble. But take heart! I have overcome the world." (John 16:33)

Also: Isaiah 26:3; John 14:27; Psalm 29:11

Recovering from surgery or illness:

"May the God of hope fill you with all joy and peace as you trust in him, so that you may overflow with hope by the power of the Holy Spirit." (Romans 15:13)

Also: *Psalm 34:4-7, Psalm 28:7, Romans 8:28*

Sadness

"The Lord is close to the broken hearted and saves those who are crushed in spirit." (Psalm 34:18)

Also: Matthew 5:4; Psalm 147:3; John 14:1; Psalm 18:2

Seeking guidance

"If any of you lacks wisdom, you should ask God, who gives generously to all without finding fault, and it will be given to you." (James 1:5)

Also: Matthew 7:24, Isaiah 40:28, Hebrews 4:16

BIBLE PASSAGES TO COMFORT AND ENCOURAGE

Strength and courage

"Do you not know? Have you not heard? The LORD is the everlasting God, the Creator of the ends of the earth. He will not grow tired or weary, and his understanding no one can fathom. He gives strength to the weary and increases the power of the weak. Even youths grow tired and weary, and young men stumble and fall; but those who hope in the LORD will renew their strength. They will soar on wings like eagles; they will run and not grow weary, they will walk and not be faint." (Isaiah 40:28-31)

Also: Philippians 4:13; 1 Chronicles 16:11; Exodus 15:2; Psalm 73:26

CHAPTER 21

PRAYERS TO SHARE

*P*raying aloud for and, perhaps, with the people you visit is a key piece of your role as a visitation ministry volunteer. Here are some tips about how to go about it.

Don't assume you know how the patient feels about God

If you're visiting someone from your congregation you might assume that the person has made a faith commitment and loves God. And you might very well be wrong.

Going to church doesn't necessarily make someone a believer. And in the face of a cancer diagnosis or traumatic accident, the person you're visiting might be actively angry with God. After all, God could have kept the cells from multiplying or pulled the car safely out of a skid. The *last* person some patients want to talk to is God. They're *furious* with him.

Which makes this second tip all that much more important.

Always ask for permission to pray

There's no need to belabor this; simply say, "If it's okay with you I'd like to pray for you and your situation." If the patient isn't agreeable with your intention to pray, you'll hear about it and can adjust accordingly.

Asking for permission is a matter of respect. You're letting the patient set the agenda. That level of respect opens the doors to deeper conversations.

Should someone say, "no," pause and then say, "I'll respect your decision but I'm wondering why you made it. Can you help me understand?" Notice that you're not challenging the patient's choice. You're seeking to understand, and that may lead to an entirely new awareness of the patient's spiritual condition.

Inquire: Is there something specific you should mention?

As Chaplain Funk discovered when a woman told him what was *really* on her mind was a family issue, not her health challenges, it pays to ask up front what's burdening a patient.

You may be asked to pray for a distressed spouse. For frightened children. For a job to still be waiting when the patient finally leaves the hospital. You don't know (and won't know) until you ask. Whatever you hear, be sure to focus on it in your prayer.

Be careful who you're talking to

You probably have a default way to address God but not every default setting is necessarily appropriate in every setting.

If you're praying with a woman who has suffered at the hands of an abusive father, you'd be wise to avoid launching into your prayer with "Heavenly Father." Why? Because the woman you're praying for may not be able to join in with you in the prayer; the word "father" has too much pain attached to allow that.

Calling God "the Great Physician," which would seem completely appropriate in a sick room, may also carry negative connotations depending on what sort of medical care a patient has received. Do this instead: open your prayer with "Dear God," or simply "God." You're not insulting God, and you're avoiding possible mishaps.

Don't perform

For some, public prayer has a language and cadence all its own. There's a sense of theatricality in phrasing and delivery. Avoid that. Make your prayer intimate and direct. You're praying from the heart and in real time; there's no need to impress.

Speak gently

Be aware of the volume and tone of your voice. If you're a natural born "boomer," your voice carrying as if it was shot out through a foghorn, you'll need to rein it in. Loud noises can startle both the patient you're visiting and any other patients or staff within earshot.

If you tend to speak softly, turn up your volume slightly. Make it easy for a patient to hear you without straining.

If you're not sure how your voice is being received, before praying, carry on a conversation and ask, "Can you hear me comfortably? Would you like me to speak either more softly or louder?" Apply the answer you get to how you modulate your prayer, too.

Be sensitive to the Holy Spirit's leading and what to pray for

Some intercessory prayer proponents point out Jesus' words, "everything is possible if you believe "(Mark 9:23) and maintain that faithfully asking for a cure gives God a clear pathway to provide one.

Others say that God will do what God will do, prayer or no prayer. That in prayer we're attempting to cooperate with his purposes, not broker a desired outcome.

And others caution that the healing God may have in mind for a patient isn't necessarily physical, that the outcome God may most desire is that the person be healed spiritually or emotionally. After all, physical death isn't the worst thing that can happen to a believer.

While various churches and denominations take different approaches to prayer, its practice, importance, and power is something we as Christ-followers hold in common. If uncertain as to what or how to pray, a simple option is to follow Christ's lead from the Lord's prayer (Matthew 6:9-13).

Include others in the room

Be they family, friends, or caregivers, if the patient says it's okay to pray, do so inclusively. Other visitors or staff won't contradict the patient. That said, it's still respectful to ask if the others present wish to be included. You may discover that they specifically don't want to be included for reasons they aren't eager to share.

Whatever boundaries they set, respect them. You don't know what's behind those boundaries, although should the opportunity arise later outside the room, you can gently ask. You can, in a sentence of two, mention the others. "Give those who are providing care wisdom and endurance" covers caregivers, and "Give peace to those who are concerned for John" covers John's family, friends, and colleagues.

Keep it short

Some say that a two-minute prayer is about right, but don't feel the need to go that long. You're inviting God into the room, and it's an invitation God is eager to accept. You needn't implore or stir up passion; you're helping a patient who's in a swirl of emotion focus on the God who can heal and restore.

Pray briefly, then wrap up.

Consider including some or all of the Lord's Prayer (Matthew 6:9-13)

These are often comforting words even for those whose last experience with faith or church happened decades before. Especially if you're calling on someone from your congregation and the Lord's

Prayer is a regular part of your liturgy, you may find the patient is praying aloud along with you.

Linger

Many visitors pray as they're heading out the door, but consider allowing time in your visit to remain in the room awhile. Here's why: prayer often lays bare emotions that a patient has kept hidden. Tears that were held back course down cheeks, a voice that was steady and nonchalant before the prayer shakes with emotion. If that happens, gently invite exploration with, "It seems that praying has touched you in some way. I'm wondering how—and if that's something you'd be willing to talk about."

Ask for permission to keep praying once you're home—*if* you intend to do so

The world is full of empty promises to pray for others. If your intent is to keep praying once your visit is over, ask if that's okay and then *do it*. Keeping a person in prayer softens your heart for that person and will often lead to more authentic prayers…and a sincere desire to reconnect with the person.

But don't say you'll pray and then fail to do it. It's not just a matter of integrity. There's a spiritual dynamic at work, too.

The most meaningful prayers are those that spring from your own heart. That said, here are some sample prayers to help provide you with examples and language you might found helpful in certain instances.

Prayers for comfort

Dear God,
You're the source of comfort, strength, and hope. We ask that
you pour out all those, that we experience peace. Give us

all your strength to meet the challenges that lay ahead. We know we're not alone, that you walk with us; help us feel your loving presence.
Amen

God,
We put ourselves in your hands. You've promised to be our guide, our comfort, and our refuge—help us feel the truth in your promises.
Give us the faith to set aside anxiety and instead trust you.
Thank you for walking through these coming hours with us.
Amen.

God,
Thank you that you don't love us just from afar.
That when we hurt, you hurt along with us.
That when we cry, you taste the salt in our tears.
That when we're afraid, you lean in close to reassure us.
That when we hope, it's your hope that's alive within us.
Be especially close to (patient) and all your children today.
Stay close—we need you.
Amen

Prayers for rest

Dear God,
I pray that my friend (patient) find rest today.
That (patient) experience the physical rest (s)he needs, and the emotional rest that comes from knowing (s)he's in your hands.
Quiet his/her spirit and set his/her mind at ease.
Amen.

God,
You're the God of a peace that passes understanding.
We ask for that peace today. May it settle into this room and touch not just (patient) but all who are intent on bringing help and healing into his/her life.
We love you and trust you. Help us all cling to the hope that's in you and you alone.
Amen.

Prayers for caregivers

Dear God,
We pray for those who will care for (patient) while (s)he's here.
Give them wisdom as they go about their work, and compassion that reassures and comforts the patients they serve.
Be with them, work through them, and bring your healing to all they touch.
Amen.

God,
Thank you for the care (patient) is receiving.
We pray for those who give it, from the doctors and medical staff to the administrators to the nutritionists; all the professionals who give care around the clock.
Give them sharp minds and skills, and walk with them as they do their work.
Work through them, God.
Amen.

Prayers with families in waiting rooms

Dear God,
Be with (patient) and also with those attending to him/her.

Give (patient's) caregivers wisdom and skill. Work through them, God.

And work in our hearts, God. Give us peace and the wisdom to trust you.

Thank you for your promise to be with (patient) and with us.

Amen.

God,

We ask for courage to face these hard hours. Grant us the faith to trust you and in your love for (patient). We know you are with him/her.

Also be with us. May your presence fill our hearts, driving out fear.

Amen.

Prayers in crises

Dear God,

So much is happening right now. Give us clear minds and hearts that trust you.

We ask for that peace that passes understanding because there's so much we don't understand in this moment.

Help us see you, hear you, and trust you.

Amen.

God,

We know you're with us even in this hard time.

So speak to us, and speak clearly. We need to hear from you. We need to see you at work. We need to live in hope rather than in fear.

We love you and we're yours. Be with us now.

Amen.

Prayers in the face of imminent death

Dear God,

In you there is no shadow, no darkness.

You know (patient) and (s)he knows you. Draw (patient) to you and calm his/her heart during these hours.

Welcome him/her home, God, in your good time and your right way.

We praise you for your love and thank you for your grace.

And be with us as we lean on you now.

Amen.

God,

Thank you for the promise of life in you, life that stretches out into eternity.

Welcome (patient) into that life. And comfort our hearts as we trust in you and your perfect will.

This isn't easy for us, God. We rely on you and the hope that's in you.

Amen.

Prayers of celebration

Dear God,

Thank you for the good news—that (patient) is on the road to recovery.

We know that all good news—all good gifts—are from you. The good news about (patient) and the good news that through the gift of Jesus we can be your friends.

Thanks, friend, for this spirit-lifting, joyful update.

Amen.

God,

A new baby! Thank you for the miracle of new life, and the good news that all here who had a part in ushering this new life into this world are doing well.

We welcome this little one with open arms—just like you welcome us.

Thank you, God. Thank you from the bottom of our joy-filled hearts.

Amen.

A prayer inviting Jesus into one's life

Lead the person who's inviting Jesus into his or her life in a prayer like the following:

Dear Jesus,

It's true--I'm a sinner, and I need and want your forgiveness.

I believe you died for my sins and rose from the dead.

I'm sorry for the wrong I've done and with your help turn from my sins.

And I invite you into my life, Jesus, as my lord and savior.

I'm all in, Jesus. I'm all yours.

Amen.

CHAPTER 22

SELF-CARE

*J*esus said the poor would be with us always (Matthew 26:11) and he could have easily said the same thing about the sick and dying, which means your ministry is a marathon, not a sprint. You need to take care of yourself so you can remain effective.

Compassion fatigue is a common occurrence among those who are frequently asked to respond to the needs of others. The well eventually runs dry; what was a passion for service becomes a duty, then an obligation, and then an activity that's abandoned.

Visitors simply burn out and leave their ministry behind.

Hopefully, whoever organizes your congregation's visitation ministry has in place a strategy to counter fatigue and burnout. But even if that's the case, it's up to you to take your emotional and spiritual pulse to determine if you're in danger.

Are you exhausted? Increasingly impatient or demanding? Do you feel unappreciated by those you visit and those who send you on a visit? Is depression or an inability to sleep well plaguing you? Your service as a visitor may not be responsible for any of those difficulties if they appear in your life, but it's worth making sure by combating burnout in these ways:

Talk about your visits

Share with the ministry coordinator or another visitor what went well, what went poorly, and how you might be better prepared moving forward. Be transparent: there's no shame if a visit blew up or fizzled out. Learn together and move on.

Take a hike

Literally, not figuratively. Listening is grueling work, and the better shape you're in, the more you're able to handle the challenge. Increase your physical exercise and make wise choices about what and when you eat. Your stamina will improve.

Grow spiritually through worship

Maybe it's singing and maybe it's not. However you connect with God, be intentional about doing it frequently. Invite God to speak into your life and take seriously your discipleship. You're asking him to speak to you while you're making a visit; be sure you can tell his voice from your own.

Jesus said if you abide in him you'll be able to do much (John 15:4).

You can't do this ministry on your own so don't try.

Set healthy boundaries

You may discover you can't handle three calls in a week. If that's the case, let your ministry coordinator know what you can handle emotionally and stick with it. Don't let yourself walk out of a room where someone's suffering carrying the weight of that suffering yourself.

Jim Stiles, a crisis center trainer in Michigan, put it this way: "All the troubled people you encounter are carrying monkeys on their backs. You come along to talk about their problems and it's easy for the monkeys to jump on your back. The troubled people are less troubled but you're weighed down. Collect a couple of monkeys and you'll be of no use to anyone any longer. Make sure the monkeys stay where they are. It's the only way you'll survive."

Reflect—in writing

Journaling can help you identify your thoughts and feelings about time spent with someone who's suffering or dying. You'll come to know what triggers your emotions, and what thoughts lead you to dark or light places.

Get a massage

Let someone work the stress out of your neck, back, and shoulders. Being kind to yourself following a tough visit may be just what it takes to keep you in the fight.

CHAPTER 23

DISCUSSION QUESTIONS

*Y*ou'll deepen your skills and grow closer as a team as you discuss the following questions together as a ministry team.

Section 1 Questions

After introducing yourselves and sharing stories about any recent visits, talk about this:

• Why have you chosen to serve in the visitation ministry? What's a story from your life that helps shed light on your decision?

• Which Bible passage in chapter 2 speaks most loudly to you? Why?

• Tell about a time someone quickly connected with you in a deep way. In what ways did listening play a role?

• How's the fit of your heart for this ministry? Your stomach? Your spirit?

Section 2 Questions

After sharing stories about any recent visits, discuss:

• What sort of listener are you? Give an example of why you answer as you do.

• Tell about a time someone comforted you in a meaningful way. What did that person say or do that mattered most?

Section 3 Questions

After sharing stories about any recent visits, discuss:

• Which practical suggestion about hospital visits surprised you?

• On a scale of one to ten, how comfortable are you visiting a nursing home? Explain why you answer as you do.

• What's the best piece of advice you see in the In-Home Visits chapter?

• If the opportunity to lead someone to Christ arose in the context of a visit, how would you do it? What would you say?

• What piece of advice given do you want to keep in mind the next time you visit with an elderly person, or a person who's terminally ill?

CHAPTER 24

RECOMMENDED RESOURCES

*A*mong the many different *Chicken Soup for the Soul* books, there are several upbeat, appropriate titles for visitors to carry with them on visits to nursing homes and home settings. Among them are *Think Positive*, *A Book of Miracles*, *Heartwarming Stories About People 60 and Over*, and *Older & Wiser: Stories of Inspiration, Humor, and Wisdom*.

Listening for Heaven's Sake (Anne Clippard, David Ping, David W. Sweeten) and *Quick to Listen Leaders* (Dave Ping and Anne Clippard) from Equipping Ministries International (equippingministries.org) teach practical listening skills in a Christian context.

Listening and Caring Skills: A Guide for Groups and Leaders by (John S. Savage, 1996, Abingdon Press) provides practical insight into 11 specific listening skills—all of which will help you listen with greater depth and compassion.

Caring Enough to Hear and Be Heard (David W. Augsburger, Regal Books, 1982,) is a classic—and targets creating listening and sharing skills.

Visit the Sick: Ministering God's Grace in Times of Illness (Brian Croft, Zondervan, 2014) covers visitation basics crisply and clearly.

Coming Alongside (Jeffrey R. Funk) explores the biblical foundation of the visitation and care ministry, and distills decades of experience into an easily accessible 200 pages. A must-read.

The Listening Life (Adam S. McHugh, Intervarsity Press, 2015) provides a deep dive into developing a listening lifestyle, with attention paid to listening to people in pain.

Stephen Ministries is a faith-based organization providing training and resources for caring ministries, spiritual gift discovery, grief support, and spiritual growth. [stephenministries.org; (314)-428-2600]

A Compassionate Visitation Program For Church Homebound Elders by Julia Quiring Emblen is an online course (2.5 contact hours) helping churches create excellent visitation ministries. Specific tips from a medical perspective are shared.

ABOUT THE CONTRIBUTORS

*J*t shouldn't come as a surprise that people who generously give of themselves to visit those who are sick and struggling are also generous with sharing their expertise, insight, and stories. Among those who shared with you through the pages of this manual are:

Jeffrey R. Funk is the former Executive Director of the Healthcare Chaplains Ministry Association. He's taught Pastoral Care and Chaplaincy at Talbot School of Theology, and served as a hospital, police, and Boy Scouts of America chaplain. In the course of his career he's visited with countless patients and their families.

Maura Barrett is the Pastoral Care Associate at St. Thomas Parish in Delmar, New York. As a Licensed Master Social Worker and Senior Care Adviser she brings both professional insight and a passionate heart to both visiting and directing a team of pastoral visitors.

Sue Blagg has served with Saddleback Church's Pastoral Care Team since 2004 and is a vital link between incoming requests for visits and a Saddleback visitor showing up in a hospital room. What does she consider essential for success as a visitor? Compassion is what fuels the visiting engine.

Rob Strouse is a retired pastor in Colorado. In his decades of ministry Rob earned the reputation of being the "visiting guy" in congregations he served. The best advice he received as a young youth minister being trained by his mentor: "don't sit on the bed."

Kerri Loesche has more than 20 years' experience dealing with visitors in a nursing home setting. She's seen it all, and her advice about how to be a visitor who's welcome back is invaluable.

And thanks to this cast of characters whose insight shaped this book: Doctor Tom, David, Devon, Susan, Ken, Mike, Matt, Jenn, Dana, Dan, Ed, DeAnne, Lacey, Helen, Tricia, and Jim.

Due to the personal nature of their stories, some names of people in this list have been changed to ensure confidentiality

Writer

Mikal Keefer is a Christian writer who has published more than 35 books for children, youth, and adults, as well as writing for a wide array of magazines and curriculums. He's also visited in hospitals, homes, homeless shelters, dorms, prisons, and nursing facilities. And to those of us who have had the privilege of working with him, he's both an editorial pro and a prankster.

General Editor

Matt Lockhart spent more than twenty-five years serving in a variety of editorial and leadership roles in Christian publishing at Serendipity House, Group, and Standard/David C Cook. With a penchant for product development, he continues to enjoy helping to create Kingdom focused resources like the *Outreach Ministry Guides*.

Names   Phone and Email

_____   _____

_____   _____

_____   _____

_____   _____

_____   _____

_____   _____

_____   _____

_____   _____

_____   _____

How Can a Prayer Ministry Transform Your Church?

Whether you are part of your church's prayer ministry, or thinking about starting or joining a prayer ministry team, the *Prayer Ministry Volunteer Handbook* is for you!

We are often very quick to say we will pray for someone when we hear they are going through tough times, but do we actually follow through with our promise to pray for them? How many times do we turn to prayer only in times of crisis, as a last resort, or simply to ask things of God?

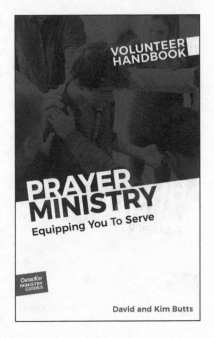

We need to make prayer the first course of action, guiding all of our life decisions. We must challenge ourselves to move beyond the dinnertime and bedtime prayers and progress to a thoughtful conversation with Christ.

Join authors David and Kim Butts as they explore how a well-equipped church prayer ministry team can serve as a model and an encouragement to support the members of the congregation, and even the pastoral staff, in their prayer journeys. Discover how you can make your church a house of prayer for all believers.

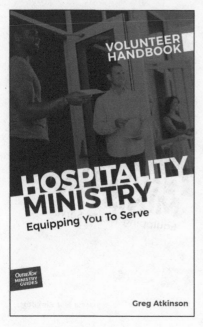

Be Our Guest

Whether you are a volunteer in your church's guest services ministry, or thinking about serving alongside ushers, greeters, welcome desk hosts, and parking lot attendants at your church, the *Hospitality Ministry Volunteer Handbook* is for you!

How does a member of community see your church? When they hear your church's name, what is their initial reaction? We want any individual who steps foot onto our church campus to immediately feel Christ's love through our actions toward them—the question is, are we doing a good job at accomplishing that mission?

We might not think of customer service and church hospitality in the same vein, but this book shows how a service mentality can make life-changing first impressions on newcomers. It's filled with specific, practical strategies and tools to help the hospitality ministry team show the love of Christ to every visitor.

Join author Greg Atkinson as he helps identify ways your church can increase its hospitality to the community around you, and, ultimately, reach those people for the Kingdom of God.

Practical Outreach Ideas and Ministry Tools

Never has there been a greater need to share the good news of God's love with those in our communities. This compact handbook shows how individual Christians and ministry teams can share the gospel by reaching out to and serving others.

Featuring 121 outreach ideas, this book helps to equip ministry teams with practical tools to serve families, children, youth, seniors, first responders, the oppressed and under resourced, millennials, single parents, local schools and businesses and more!

Designed for ministry volunteers, the book is a compact handbook of outreach ministry helps, which in addition to the dozens of outreach ideas also include outreach Scriptures and prayers, ways to share your faith, team discussion questions and recommended outreach ministries and resources.

This helpful little book is a great resource for equipping outreach ministry volunteers to serve others and to share the good news!

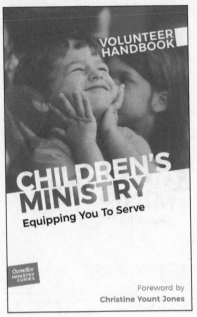

VOLUNTEER HANDBOOK

CHILDREN'S MINISTRY
Equipping You To Serve

Foreword by
Christine Yount Jones

Equipping Children's Ministry Volunteers

Whether you are part of your church's children's ministry, or thinking about serving in children's ministry, the *Children's Ministry Volunteer Handbook* is for you!

Too often, people view children's ministry as a place to drop off the kids so the adults can listen to the sermon, uninterrupted. They fail to see the power and potential of children's ministry.

In Matthew 19:13-14, Jesus said, "Let the little children come to me, and do not hinder them, for the kingdom of heaven belongs to such as these." While we may see the naivete of children as a detriment, Jesus sees it as a strength—there is beauty in the simplicity of the gospel. Investing in children's ministry is a worthwhile and crucial part of the church.

This practical handbook features insights from six authors, all experts in the field of children's ministry, with over 100 years of combined experience. They will help guide you through the challenges and joys of children's ministry—and how it is vital to the Kingdom of God.

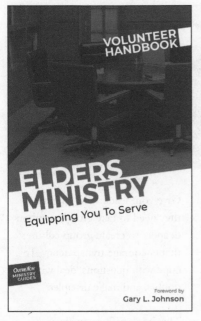

Biblical Guidance and Practical Advice for Church Elders and Prospective Elders

Equip church elders to lead well. More than better methods, the church today needs better leaders. But too often we recruit these leaders (the New Testament calls them *elders*) without equipping them for their vital task. This practical handbook presents the need, lifts up the Bible's vision for elder ministry, and provides a wealth of practical how-to training to help elders provide the spiritual leadership that can't come from anyone else. Elder teams will build unity and confidence as they discuss it together.

Written by the ministry founders and leaders of e2: effective elders, content is based on decades of local-church experience and interaction with everyday elders in hundreds of congregations.

VOLUNTEER HANDBOOK

SMALL GROUP MINISTRY

Equipping You To Serve

Outreach MINISTRY GUIDES

Mikal Keefer

Equip Small Group Leaders to Lead Well

Your church's small group ministry is where faith can get real. Where masks can slide off and honest struggles and doubts surface.

Maybe. It all depends on the leaders of your groups.

Give your leaders the training they need to take group members deeper. To create group cultures that encourage transparency. To cope with questions, deal with doubts, and make disciples.

This book offers your team a lifetime of easy-to-read, easy-to-remember advice from experienced small group ministry leaders. They share what they've learned, what they wish they'd known earlier, and dozens of proven practical tips that will aid in developing healthy small groups in your church.

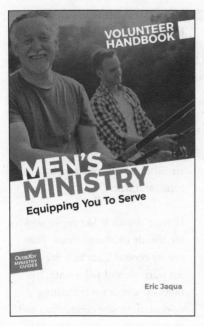

A men's ministry that guys will look forward to being a part of!

Every church wants to actively engage and grow men—but most men's ministries have a hard time getting guys in the door. This wildly practical ministry handbook equips men's ministry volunteers and their leaders with proven suggestions for building a program that's magnetic to men.

Give your ministry team the tools, tips, and training they need to help develop the trust and accountability between men which leads to deep, lasting spiritual growth.

Included within this helpful men's ministry guide:

- Practical ways to get men into the Word
- Guidance for effective men's group meetings
- Dozens of ideas for serving together, fostering accountability, strengthening family connections, and more!

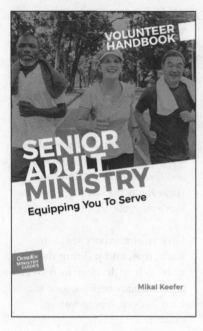

Take your Senior Adult Ministry to the Next Level

That's what will happen when you train and equip your Senior Adult Ministry volunteers not just to minister to seniors, but also to minister *with* them. Help deepen seniors' faith and grow their friendships with one another, your team, and with God.

If your church is like most, seniors are mostly on the sidelines, but not by choice! They're hungry for purpose and fellowship. But unless you're actively creating opportunities for connection and contribution, many senior adults feel unneeded and unwelcome and simply drop out.

In this Outreach Ministry Guide you'll discover:
- Dozens of senior-friendly programming ideas
- Guidance and biblical wisdom for helping seniors cope with change, loneliness, and grief
- Ideas for energizing senior adult Sunday school classes, senior-sized service projects, and more!